SNOW

The Rise and Fall of a Medellin Drug Pilot

by William Norris

Norris, William
ISBN: 0-7443-0291-9
Snowbird/William Norris – 1st ed.

SynergEbooks
1235 Flat Shoals Rd
King, NC 27021
www.SynergEbooks.com

Graphics Design for cover by Barbara Quanbeck
Contact the author via email at mandychops@ukonline.co.uk

Other titles by William Norris:

A Grave Too Many
The Man Who Fell From the Sky
The Badger Game
Willful Misconduct

Available in paperback and in eBook format at
SynergEbooks
1235 Flat Shoals Rd
King, NC 27021
http://www.SynergEbooks.com

SNOWBIRD

CHAPTER ONE

Even before the pig flew over the windshield, Andrew Barnes knew he had made a mistake.   This was not the runway he was looking for.   It wasn't a runway at all. The brown strip rushing towards him in the landing lights of the twin-engined Rockwell Turbo-Commander was nothing more than a rutted country lane.   The flickering lights that he had taken as threshold markers were actually the headlamps of an ancient truck, jolting along and minding its own business.

"Oh, shit," said Andrew Barnes.

There was no going back.   Flaps extended, nose high, the Turbo-Commander was committed to landing.   The engines screamed in fine pitch as they swallowed the last few gallons of fuel in the tanks.   The stall-warning horn blared in protest.   On the ground, an astonished Colombian farmer stood on his brakes and lurched into a ditch as the monstrous shape skimmed the roof of his truck and struck the road only yards ahead.

"Hang on tight," shouted Barnes.   Paralysed with fear, his two passengers hardly needed to be told.   With a spine-jarring jolt the main wheels touched and stayed down as the fully-stalled aircraft fell out of the sky.   The nose dropped, and they watched with horrified fascination through the windshield as the Turbo-Commander began a wild charge down the track.   Barnes fought for control, stabbing at brakes and rudder pedals, miraculously dodging the trees and bushes that flashed past the wingtips. And then the road turned. There was nowhere to go.

The aircraft left the path, crossed a ditch, smashed through a hedge, and hurled itself into a farmyard. Startled chicken scattered in all directions.

And a pig flew over the windshield.

With a final expensive crunch, the Turbo-Commander plunged its nose into a wooden fence. And stopped.

*   *   *   *

Andrew Barnes told me that story on the first day we met. It was not a chance encounter. Some three weeks before I had had a telephone call from Michael Knipe, then Foreign News Editor of The Times. Michael, an old friend from my own days with that once-distinguished newspaper, was calling to do me a favour. At least, he hoped it was going to be a favour. He sounded a trifle nervous.

The Times man in New York, said Michael, had just been interviewing an odd character who was one of the witnesses in the cocaine-smuggling trial of Carlos Lehder, down in Miami. The witness was an Englishman, now living in Pennsylvania, who had an extraordinary tale to tell about the cocaine-smuggling business. Furthermore, he seemed to want it converted into a book, and had asked the New York correspondent if he knew any good authors who might be interested. The message had been passed on to the Foreign Desk, and Michael had thought of me. Nice of him.

"What do you know about this guy?" I asked. Not a lot, it turned out. Just that his name was Barnes, that he had smuggled large quantities of cocaine for the Medellin Cartel, and he was probably heading for a lengthy spell in prison. From the sound of it, he deserved no less.

At this point I knew no more about the Medellin Cartel than the next man; merely what I had read in the press and seen on television. But it was enough to induce revulsion. By all accounts, these were unscrupulous crooks who had poisoned a continent and amassed a king's ransom in the process. On the way, they had murdered scores of men who attempted to expose their conspiracy. And some of those men, I now remembered with an odd churning in the pit of my stomach, had been journalists. From the tone of Michael's voice, clear across four thousand miles, I could tell he was thinking the same thing.

"Just thought you might be interested," he said rather lamely. "I've got his telephone number if you want it."

Why not? There was no harm in having the option. I scribbled down the number and sat looking at it pensively long after our conversation ended. I wondered about the personality of the man who lay behind that number, and I wondered even more about his associates. I had never met a drug smuggler; at least, not knowingly. Curiosity did battle with prudence, and for the moment, prudence won. I pushed the slip of paper to one side and got on with the rest of my life.

It was not a good time for authoring in the Norris household. In spite of splendid reviews for my last book and the sale of the film rights to Hollywood, there was no prospect of a commission for the next one. I was caught in the usual dilemma of the non-fiction writer: no publisher will sign a contract and pay an advance without a fully researched outline of the project. But research involves time and travel, and time and travel cost money. That money ought to come from the publisher's advance - it is what advances are supposed to be for - but in practice you cannot get one without laying out large amounts of your own cash long before you see the cheque. Which is fine if you have it. It was not the first time I had been in this Catch-22 situation, but try as I might I could find no way out of it. I ought, I thought, to give up the non-fiction trade and write novels instead. The trouble was, I was not very good at fiction.

My passion of the moment was the Lindbergh kidnapping case. Others, notably Ludovic Kennedy in his excellent book *The Airman and the Carpenter,* had proved conclusively that Bruno Richard Hauptmann was innocent of the crime, but no one had yet been able to identify the true guilty party. I believed I had a clue to his identity through newly-discovered evidence, but believing it and proving it were two very different things.

For months, I had been chasing phantoms and spending money I could ill afford in pursuit of the final truth. I had even flown to Scotland to interview Betty Gow, the Lindbergh baby's still-surviving nursemaid, only to have the door literally slammed in my face. In the United States, too, hostility and evasion were greeting every enquiry. I knew I was on the right trail, and that given sufficient time and money, persistence would pay off in the end. Time, I had. Money was a different matter. As the days passed and the crock of gold at the end of my investigatory rainbow grew no closer, I found my eyes drawn more and more to the scrap of paper lying on my desk, and the telephone number of Andrew Richard Barnes. Perhaps, after all, it was time to face reality; to put the Lindbergh project on the back burner and to tackle something that, on the face of it, looked straightforward. Something, moreover, that ought not to cost an arm and a leg to research.

My long-suffering agent in New York was mildly encouraging. My wife, faced with the prospect of her middle-aged husband associating with ruthless criminals, was appalled. Four years of exposure to American television violence did not help. "These people are worse than the Mafia," she said. "You could get yourself killed."

With some asperity, I pointed out that I had survived more dangerous assignments in the past. I had been under fire in Biafra, Zimbabwe, Angola and Mozambique.

I had been in the thick of the Paris riots in May 1968. By comparison, the prospect of rubbing shoulders with a drug smuggler was pretty small beer.

"You were younger and sillier then," she said.

That did it. I rooted out the scrap of paper and made the call.

Barnes seemed agreeable enough on the telephone, and more than willing to meet with me. The time and place could be of my choosing. I pondered the question. Aside from the fact that his house in Pennsylvania was a three-hour drive from my home in Virginia's Shenandoah Valley, did I really want to stick my head in the lion's mouth at this first meeting? At least my own place boasted three large and faithful dogs of fearful mien, plus, as a last resort, the family firearm. There was the small problem of persuading my wife to accept a drug-smuggler as a houseguest but I hoped, correctly as it turned out, that curiosity might win the day.

"Come for the week-end," I said.

During the intervening days, Betty and I speculated on what our guest would look like. Suave and sinister was the consensus of opinion. Probably slim and dark-suited, with a palpable air of menace. We were certainly unprepared for the shy giant of a man who unfolded himself from an ancient Ford Mustang in our driveway on that Saturday in late April.

Andrew Barnes was big. Very big. He looked down at us from a height of six foot three, and his chest strained at the buttons of his jacket.   There was some surplus fat there to be sure, but a hell of a lot of muscle underneath it. The   face was bucolic.   It was the sort of face that belonged on an English farm labourer, not on a drug smuggler.   The eyes were blue and, God damnit, they had a sort of innocence about them.

Barnes came towards us, a battered leather case in one hand, brushing the hair from his eyes with the other.   He wore it long with a pronounced fringe, as though in memory of the Beatles, and I became aware that the dogs had stopped barking.   They were crowding round him, sniffing his legs and showing every sign of pleasure as he bent down to pat them.   Great, I thought.   The one time I invite a criminal to my home, and you silly bastards fawn all over him.   But they were right.   For all that he had done, and it was plenty, there was no harm, no violence in Andrew Barnes.   A dog's judgment is not often wrong.

We shook hands, and I made a mental note that his grip was firm and dry.   The hands themselves, though, were surprisingly small.   Smaller than my own.   It was as though they had stopped growing in his early teens, while the rest of his physique burgeoned into manhood. It was not the only thing about Andrew Barnes, I was to discover, that betokened arrested development.

His voice, too, was a surprise.   I had expected an English accent, perhaps similar to my own.   But what came out was a sort of mid-Atlantic twang, neither one thing nor the other, but more American than not. His speech, like his whole manner, was diffident. Courteous and gentlemanly - an odd word to use in this context, but totally appropriate - but with a sheepish air about him. As we stumbled through the formalities and finally sat down in my study to begin the first of many interviews, I came to realise that he was more nervous than I. Every few seconds he would take a comb and pass it through his perfectly-ordered hair, like an errant schoolboy facing his headmaster and wondering what to do with his hands.

But he could talk. Oh my, how he could talk. At first, as names and dates and places poured out in an unrelenting stream, I began to wonder if he was not too articulate. Was it possible that this was a well-rehearsed tale being recounted for my benefit; a fictional farrago concocted with the object of making big bucks out of the book? If so, I thought wryly, this guy is singularly ignorant about the rewards of authorship, let alone the Son of Sam laws.

Slowly, I came to realise two things. First, his astonishing power of recall was largely due to the fact that he had just spent weeks and months being grilled by agents from the F.B.I. and the U.S. Drug Enforcement Agency, not to mention sundry lawyers while he stood on the witness stand in Miami.

Second, and more important, Andrew Barnes was using me as a confessor. In terms of his atonement, going to jail and paying the price was not enough. He was inwardly driven to tell the story of his misdeeds in the utmost detail to the widest possible audience. There was no altruism in it. He was not out to educate the young and prevent them falling into the same trap.

At root, he neither knew nor cared whether his revelations would have any effect on the long-term future of the drug trade. All that mattered to Andrew Barnes at this point in time was to get the whole thing off his chest so that he might, one day, make a fresh start. In short, he needed to cleanse his soul.

I am no psychologist, still less a priest, and the reader must judge as the story unfolds whether such a public *mea culpa* is justified. When it comes to evil intent, having got to know Andrew Barnes rather well, I will vouch for the fact that he is not in the same league as the man he met on a Florida airfield on December 26, 1977...

CHAPTER TWO

"Call me Joe," said the handsome young Colombian who greeted Barnes at Fort Lauderdale airport. It was not his real name. That, he said, was Rubin Montes. That, too, was a lie, but on that day, Andrew Barnes could not have cared less. Barnes was 20 years old with a wife, a baby son, and an ancient C.46 cargo plane that was eating him alive.

He was very, very broke. The important thing about Mr. Rubin Montes was not his name or his veracity, but the fifty hundred-dollar bills he was offering for Andrew's services, with the promise of much more to come.

It had been a long time since Barnes had held that sort of money. He knew what he had to do for it, and that was fine with him. To fly down to Colombia, pick up a load of marijuana and return, seemed no big deal. Everyone was doing it. True, it was technically illegal, but that only mattered if you got caught. And Andrew, who knew a dozen ways of flying into Florida undetected, had no intention of getting caught. If the morality of drug smuggling bothered his conscience, it was a small voice and quickly stilled. At that moment in time, pursued by creditors and with bankruptcy looming, Andrew Barnes would have struck a deal with the devil.

Which, in a way, is precisely what he did.

The name of the devil's agent was Charlie Bush, a rogue and scoundrel of the old school. To young Andrew Barnes, the 65 years old Charlie was a romantic father-figure; a self-taught pilot from the barnstorming days, who made his fortune wheeling and dealing in old aeroplanes after World War II. He was kind to Andrew, as Fagin was kind to Oliver Twist, and whenever the flier needed help or money, the doors of Bush Aviation on the south west side of Fort Lauderdale international airport were always open.

Charlie Bush's legitimate business was extensive. At any one time, up to two hundred aircraft could be found parked on his half-mile ramp. He repaired aircraft, large or small. He sold them, chartered them, and operated a cargo business back and forth between Florida and the Bahamas and Caribbean. He had six full time employees, and sometimes as many as thirty temporary workers. For a man partially crippled by polio, it might have seemed enough to keep him busy, without engaging in anything more illicit. But not for Charlie Bush. Charlie, to quote Andrew Barnes, was "a savvy old cat."

If the young Englishman was suspicious, even before the introduction to Montes, that his benefactor was not all that he appeared, he could hardly afford to say so. His much-needed spare parts, even engines, were supplied on credit. His aircraft was fuelled on the promise of payment later. The washing facility was free. Charlie was a crook, but it didn't show. Not at first. Why, the man was a pillar of the community.   He had even signed on to a program that gave jobs to convicts on work release, acting as their parole officer.   Why no one in authority ever realised that this was akin to putting a fox in a chicken coop is one of life's greater bureaucratic mysteries.

Obligation was the name of the game.   Charlie Bush had a simple philosophy: be generous to young pilots and keep them in your debt.   One day, the debt can be called in.

For Andrew Barnes, that time came on the day after Christmas, 1977.   Some weeks before, at the urging of Charlie Bush, he had taken his old C.46 to Canada.   It was a journey of some necessity.   The C.46 had been grounded with engine trouble, denying Andrew his only means of making an honest living, and Charlie, good old Charlie, had stepped in to help.   He had guaranteed a $33,000 note to enable Barnes to buy one reconditioned engine, and borrowed the same amount on his own account to purchase a second.

Naturally, he had not done this for nothing: Andrew had to transfer the title of the aircraft to his name, and, just for good measure, Charlie slapped a $60,000 lien on it.   The sums did not add up.   Andrew nurtured the unworthy suspicion that the old man had pocketed $27,000 somewhere along the line.   But he was in no position to argue.

Still, at least the C.46 was finally airworthy again. By now, however, the bank was shouting for its money, and Charlie got wind of the fact that a repossession crew was on its way. He told Andrew to take the aeroplane to Canada, and take a lawyer with him. There was just one thing he had to do before he went - take a check ride in a pressurised Aero-Commander. Charlie gave no explanation for this odd request, and Andrew did not ask. He went ahead and did it.

The bid to save the C.46 from the clutches of the bank was successful. Barnes obtained a restraining order from the Ontario Supreme Court, and the frustrated repossession crew who had pursued him to Canada were forced to leave empty-handed.

By now it was almost Christmas, and Andrew was anxious to be home with his family. He returned to Florida, arriving in Fort Lauderdale on Christmas Day, to find a message from Charlie Bush.

"Come at once and bring your overnight bag," it said. "I've got some real good flying for you."

Andrew went next morning. His wife, Barbara, drove him to the airport that day in the decrepit van that was their only transport.

And there he met Rubin Montes.

Montes, to preserve his alias for the moment, had been referred to Charlie Bush by a friend of Charlie's named Lee Cameron from Burbank, California. Cameron ran his own fixed-base operation at Burbank, flying twin-engined Beechcrafts and DC 3's. Like many others in the aviation business, he knew that Bush was heavily involved with drug smugglers.

Though he had not been convicted at that time, (he was to go to prison in 1986, at the age of 74, after being caught with three kilograms of cocaine and $100,000 in his car) Charlie was already selling and chartering aircraft to the smuggling fraternity, servicing them, and providing crews. He was clearly the man to supply Montes' needs.

The Colombian already had an aircraft: a gaudily-painted Rockwell Turbo-Commander Shrike, with "Summit Trucking" emblazoned on the side. It was owned by Nestor Castrion, a Colombian of mixed Indian descent, and a seasoned drug smuggler whose proudest claim was the paternity of 32 children.

Castrion was to accompany Montes on the drug run, taking with him a Christmas cargo of toys for his offspring, but neither could fly the plane. They needed a pilot.

Charlie Bush sold them the services of Andrew Barnes, who had so thoughtfully been checked out on that very type of aircraft a few weeks before.

As far as Andrew was concerned, it was not a hard sell. Charlie knew the state of his finances down to the last blob of red ink. He also had good reason to believe that the young pilot would have little scruple about breaking the law.

Charlie explained the proposition: the load would be marijuana, and he would be paid $50,000. For subsequent trips, there would be an increase of $10,000 each time. The old man pushed a well-stuffed envelope across the scarred desk in his hangar office. "Give that to Barbara," he said. Andrew took the envelope to his wife, waiting in the van, and told her to count the contents.

The men drove to the other side of the airfield, where work was being carried out on the Turbo-Commander. Charlie Bush had cautiously refused to have it standing on his own ramp, in case something went wrong and he should be implicated with the smuggling operation.

There was a fourth man in the group, a certain Larry Greenberger, who was to be responsible for the Florida end of the transaction. Greenberger was to unload the marijuana and drive it away from an airstrip at De Land, some miles inland from Daytona Beach. It was all arranged.

Montes was anxious to be off, but the Turbo-Commander was not ready. Mechanics were installing a long-range tank inside the cabin to hold the 120 gallons of extra fuel necessary for the long flight, and the work was taking longer than expected.

Andrew was worried. It began to look as though they would be arriving in Colombia after dark, at which point he would be faced with the problem of landing on a small illegal airstrip of unknown location, length and surface. It was downright dangerous, and he said so, urging postponement of the trip until the next day.   His suggestion was not well received.

Montes and Greenberger began to apply pressure.   It had to be today, they said, or not at all.   Government officials and the military in Colombia had been bribed to turn a blind eye when the "merchandise" was moved out to the airstrip; the owner of the strip had been paid $100,000.   If the flight did not go ahead on schedule, all that would be wasted.   Andrew Barnes might not be wasted, but he certainly wouldn't get paid.

Barnes needed the money enough to risk his life.   "To hell with this," he said.   "We might as well go."

At 12 noon on December 26, 1977, Turbo-Commander 26 Alpha Charlie, with Andrew Barnes at the controls, rolled down the runway at Fort Lauderdale and rose into the clear Florida sky.   Barnes set his course to the south, engaged the autopilot, and settled down for the seven-hour long haul across Haiti and the Caribbean to Colombia.   Rubin Montes sat in the right hand seat, and the two men talked.

It transpired that this was not Montes' first attempt to smuggle drugs by air.   Not long before he had flown down to Santa Marta with a Californian pilot who turned out to be a heroin addict.   At regular intervals, the pilot would leave the cockpit to take a fix, frequently falling asleep at the controls.   By the time they reached Colombia he was in no condition to find the jungle airstrip, and landed instead at the commercial airport in Santa Marta.

This was risky enough, but the pilot compounded the offence by forgetting to lower the wheels, and the aircraft made a belly landing on the main runway. Both men were promptly arrested, and had to bribe their way out of jail.

This was not an encouraging story for young Andrew Barnes, already worried by the prospect of making his first arrival in the dark, but by now he was totally committed. There was no turning back.

Seven hours was what it should have taken, but headwinds cut the Turbo-Commander's speed to a scant 175 knots. Barnes flew high, then low, but he could not escape the wind. Long before the Colombian coast passed beneath them, they were flying in total darkness. Montes, sharing the cockpit in the right hand seat, showed no sign of anxiety.

"It will look like JFK down there," he told the worried pilot. "No problem, there will be plenty of lights." He made it sound like a truly professional operation.

Their destination was fourteen miles from the coastal city of Riohacha, on a heading of 220 degrees. Finding Riohacha was easy: the local airfield had a navigation beacon, and soon the lights of the town showed up clearly. Barnes told Montes to use the aircraft's VHF radio and contact the ground crew at the smuggler's airstrip. Montes began to call.

There was no reply; nothing but the crackle of static through the headphones.

By this time, Riohacha was behind them. They were boring on into blackness, two hours behind schedule, with no sign of the promised airstrip and no word from the ground. And fuel was running low. Barnes estimated that there was a scant thirty minutes of flying time remaining.

He checked the airspeed indicator and the second hand of his watch. By his reckoning, the strip should be immediately beneath them. All three men peered down. There was nothing.

Tension was now building in the cockpit. Barnes turned to Montes. "Joe," he said, "your guys aren't here. You know what happened: they were expecting us at 6 o'clock, like you said. They probably think we've crashed, or we're not going to make it today. Those guys have just wandered off."

Barnes reached a decision. His options were diminishing. He could ditch the aircraft in the sea off Riohacha, or he could land at the nearby military airport. Neither prospect was inviting. The seas off Colombia were rough, and with its high wing configuration the Turbo-Commander would have all the floating characteristics of a submarine. On the other hand, as Montes pointed out angrily, if they landed on the military field they would face instant arrest. Montes had experience of Colombian jails.   "You're not going to like it," he said.

"Give me something else, Joe," said Barnes.   For him, survival was now more important than freedom.   "We're running out of fuel, and in fifteen minutes time this crate is coming out of the sky, military airport or not.   If we go down over uncharted terrain, we are likely to lose our lives.   No, not just likely to lose them, we will lose our lives."

"Go back out there one more time," said Montes.   He was beginning to sweat.

"You've got one last shot at it," grunted Barnes. "We've got just enough juice to squeak out there and take another look."   He reversed their course towards the supposed position of the airstrip, adjusting his mixture controls to lean-off the engines as much as he dared to get every minute of flying time out of the few gallons of fuel still sloshing in the tanks.

"I'm now seriously thinking about going in the water off the beach," he said later.   "I can see from the lights of the town that here's a pier there.   The thing that makes me nervous about that is that this is an Aero Commander, and that thing goes down like a submarine.   The wings are up on top of you, and the fuselage is down low.   I didn't like the idea of setting it in the water.   But I didn't tell him that I was going to land at the military airport if it came to it, and just take my chances."

Suddenly, the two men saw a light.   Not much of a light, to be true; not much more than a flashlight.   But it was palpably flashing.   Then a second gleam appeared beside the first, flashing in unison as though someone was signaling with the headlights of a car.

"That's it,"   shouted Montes.   "That's got to be it, Andy."

Almost sick with relief, the young pilot lowered his flaps and landing gear and set up an impromptu circuit, using the lights as a reference point, on the assumption that this was the ground crew marking the threshold of the airstrip.

It was then that he landed in the farmyard.   Barnes remembered the moment ruefully.   "It was too late," he said. "I was committed to that landing. I could see it was a truck just before I flared over it, and I thought he was trying to light the strip for us. He was totally oblivious - the truck driver almost had a heart attack.   I felt the main wheels hit. I felt for sure we were about to hit trees and all that stuff, but it just didn't happen.   I had my landing lights on.   All I can remember is heavy braking and just pulling everything I could to start shutting stuff off.   I knew we were low on fuel: it would be unlikely for us to blow up unless we caught a wing tip or something and tore a wing off. But it all happened so quickly that really there was no time for reactions. When I got out of the plane my heart was doing about 200 r.p.m."

Rubin Montes was the first one out of the aircraft. A sawn-off shotgun had appeared in his hands as though by magic. Nestor Castrion, similarly armed, followed him to the ground. Barnes, the adrenaline still pumping through his veins like high-octane fuel, was shocked at the implication of violence. What the hell was he getting himself into?

"All of a sudden they've got guns now," he recalled. "They're going out of the door to find out who needs to be taken care of. I was shit-scared."

The two men disappeared into the darkness, leaving the pilot to inspect the damage with the aid of a flashlight. There was dust and mud everywhere, but all things considered, the would-be smugglers had escaped lightly. Barnes found that the nosewheel tire had been shredded in the heavy landing, rendering it completely useless. There were plenty of popped rivets and some deformation of the fuselage, and the nosewheel structure seemed a little loose.

It could have been much worse. Nevertheless, they were now stranded in the backwoods of Colombia with an unserviceable and illegal aeroplane, with no flight plan and no entry visas on their passports.

Apprehensively, Barnes calculated the likely length of their prison sentence if they were caught. At any moment he expected to hear the sound of gunfire, but within minutes Montes and Castrion had returned, smiling broadly.

"Everything's all right," said Montes. "I talked to the owner of the farm and gave him my ring to make him feel better about the pigs and chickens. He's going to help us." He waved his hand to show that the diamond ring he had been boasting about during the trip was no longer there. It had been worth, he said, $20,000.

Twenty thousand dollars buys a lot of co-operation in the backwoods of Colombia. The farmer, it transpired, had a bulldozer. He was willing to use it to convert his road into an impromptu airstrip, promising to have it ready for a dawn take-off.

"We're not going anywhere without a nosewheel," Barnes objected.

"No problem," said Montes. By this time the missing ground crew had arrived, having seen the Turbo-Commander circling the area as they returned from Riohacha and a vain attempt to find out why the 'plane was late. It transpired that three weeks before another aircraft of the same type had crashed on landing at the airstrip, three miles away. Among the salvaged parts was a perfectly serviceable nosewheel. Barnes worked through the night to fit it. At first light, he was dog-tired and depressed. "I was thinking, boy, why did I get into this mess," he said later. "I decide I am just going to go home and accept bankruptcy and all that. I really felt like a prick down there."

The feeling did not last long. At first light, reality set in once more. Barnes could see that the farmer and his bulldozer had done a good job: the impromptu runway was short - only 1,500 feet - but it was just adequate. Within the hour, with a minimum of fuel and only himself and Montes on board, Barnes had taken off in the battered Turbo-Commander and made the short hop to the airstrip he had missed the previous night.

This one, the ground crew had assured him, was a different proposition. It was 6,000 feet long. Why, they claimed, even a DC 6 had been able to land there. This was no lie. Barnes saw the burned-out wreckage of the big four-engined transport lying in the jungle as he circled to land.

He turned to Montes. "Joe," he said, "it doesn't count, just getting in here. Getting out is what matters."

"They have a weird, perverse sense of humour, those Colombians," said Barnes. "The guy had been telling me all night: `don't worry, it's a beautiful strip over there. A DC 6 has been in there.' As soon as I got there, I knew what they meant. I was walking around it. Four guys got killed in that DC 6, trying to take off. They just went running on through the bush, and I guess they took a tree through the wing root or something, and the damn thing just blew up. The four guys were buried there - what parts they could find of them."

Understandably, Barnes failed to share the joke. "I started getting scared now," he said. "These people were just totally reckless. They had no idea of what an aeroplane was; they just treated it like a truck. They would just load it up and then expect you to try to take off with it. But there was not much I could do: everyone was wearing guns around there."

Barnes looked at the rock-strewn runway, at the wreckage of the DC6, and his own damaged nosewheel assembly. It had survived the landing, but was shimmying badly. He pleaded with Montes not to allow the ground crew to put more than a thousand pounds of marijuana on board for the direct flight to De Land.

No one was listening. Bale after bale was stacked in the cabin, until the crew had to use the cockpit door to get in. In all there was about 1,500lb. Together with the extra fuel for the long haul back to Florida, that made the Turbo-Commander about 20 per cent over its permissible gross weight. There would be no hope of treating the fragile nosewheel gently - it would have to be held on the ground until well beyond normal take-off speed. Barnes considered refusing to fly, looked at the Colombians, looked at their guns, and thought better of it. He backtracked to the far end of the strip, revved the engines to maximum power, released the brakes and hoped for the best.

For long seconds, nothing much happened. The overloaded Turbo-Commander was reluctant to move. Then it began to accelerate slowly, too slowly, bouncing heavily over the uneven surface. Then, at 70 knots, the weakened nosewheel strut collapsed completely. The aircraft lurched forward and slid on its belly, rocks eating away at the fragile alloy skin until they tore great holes and began bouncing around in the cockpit.   For the second time in twelve hours, Andrew Barnes turned off every switch in sight and prayed they would not burn. He was lucky.   The Turbo-Commander came to rest in a huge cloud of dust, and the shaken crew climbed out as the Colombians advanced mournfully up the strip to unload the cargo once again.

Barnes' reaction was one of relief.   He had been convinced that the aircraft would never get off the ground; now he was rid of it.   He watched with satisfaction as Montes struck a match and torched the wreckage.   Nestor Castrion, some $250,000 poorer, felt somewhat differently.   This was becoming an expensive trip.

And it was not over yet.   The three potential smugglers were now stranded in Colombia.   Weary, and more than a little the worse for wear, they accepted the loan of a vehicle from the owner of the airstrip and began to drive north towards Barranquilla, six hours away. Riohacha would have been closer, but Riohacha had no hotel and only a vestigial telephone service.

Worse, it was a place where a gringo like Andrew Barnes (a conspicuous six foot three, and weighing 230 pounds) would be arrested on sight.   The police would have no doubt about what he had been up to.   Thanks to the generous loading habits of the Colombians, there were a lot of pilots walking around the region without aeroplanes.

Barranquilla, on the other hand, was a tourist centre with a good hotel. An American or Brit could blend into the background. First, however, they had to get there, and the coast road leading north was studded with military checkpoints where identification documents were closely examined. Barnes' British passport, of course, was devoid of Colombian entry stamps.

"No problem," said Rubin Montes. This meant, as usual, that there *was* a problem; they had simply not yet struck it. He produced his own German passport, which had entry stamps galore. "Show them that," he said. "Only, try not to show them the picture." It was a reasonable precaution. Montes was short, dark and slight, with swarthy Latin good looks. Barnes was an Anglo-Saxon hulk. Rarely can two men have looked less alike.

Andrew Barnes took the passport and looked at the name. It was then he discovered who "Rubin Montes," alias "Joe" really was - his employer was Carlos Lehder Rivas. At that point in time, the name meant nothing. It was to come to mean a great deal.

Carlos Lehder had underestimated the diligence of the Colombian military. At each of seven checkpoints on the road to Barranquilla they looked at Andrew Barnes, looked at the passport picture, and laughed. Then they ordered the pilot from the car at gunpoint and searched him thoroughly. He was very scared. Lehder and Castrion were less concerned. They knew the score, and they knew the tariff. Several hundred dollars changed hands at each checkpoint, and the trio were allowed to proceed.

In Barranquilla, they stayed at the Hotel Del Prado, right on the beach, where Lehder rented a big suite on the top floor. Money seemed to be no problem with the Colombian; he was determined to make this operation work whatever the cost, and by now the expenses were approaching half a million dollars with nothing to show for it.

Whatever qualms Andrew Barnes may have had at the outset, and they were probably few, he was now a whole-hearted member of the team. From Barranquilla he telephoned Charlie Bush to tell him that they needed another aeroplane. And Charlie, as ever, was willing to oblige. For a price.

The aircraft selected belonged to Bob Morgan, another member of the Florida smuggling fraternity, currently serving 30 years in jail. It was a Beechcraft Twin-Bonanza - the Excalibur version with 400 hp engines - and Morgan, said Charlie, was willing to hire it out for $70,000 for the single trip. It was not exactly a bargain rate: you could *buy* a second-hand Twin-Bonanza for that sort of money. But it probably reflected the risks involved. There was an even chance that Morgan would never see the aircraft again. In any case, Lehder was in no position to haggle. He arranged with Larry Greenberger to take the $70,000 in cash to Fort Lauderdale, and the Bonanza was handed over to Jack Leibolt, a friend of Andrew's, who was to ferry it down to the Riohacha airstrip.

For once the operation went smoothly. Leibolt, a vastly experienced pilot who had flown with the Englishman in more honest days, arrived dead on time and handed over the aircraft to Barnes. The latter was pleased to see it. He had flown the Beechcraft before, and thought it much better suited to this type of flying. It was more heavily built than the Turbo-Commander, with plenty of power to handle the load, and had been equipped with bladder tanks to extend the range. Jack Leibolt told him it was "running fine."

What he did not tell him, and what Barnes forgot to ask, was how to get the extra petrol from the bladder tanks into the aircraft's main fuel system. A small point, but not without importance.

Leibolt had flown in at sunset, and was quickly on his way out of the country via Barranquilla and Aruba. In the morning, as Barnes supervised the refueling of the aircraft, Carlos Lehder arrived with the "merchandise." This time, it was not bales of marijuana. Instead there were nine suitcases, some duffel bags, cardboard boxes, and an automobile fuel tank.

"What are we taking that for, Joe?" asked Barnes innocently, looking at the tank.

"Well, there's things inside it," replied Lehder.

The penny dropped. "We're going to haul cocaine, aren't we, Joe?" Barnes said.

"Shsh. Don't let anyone know."

Andrew Barnes, for the first and possibly the last time in his smuggling career, rebelled. "I don't want to haul coke, Joe!" he said. It was not a moral rebellion; he simply knew that the penalties for getting caught would be vastly greater.

"You want to get out of here, don't you?" Lehder retorted. "If we refuse to haul this load they'll probably kill us, so keep your voice down." Barnes looked at the guns and then at the faces around him. His short-lived revolt was over.

The reason for the switch, Lehder explained, was purely economic. A load of marijuana would have been worth, perhaps, $300,000. They had already spent that much on aeroplanes, let alone the other expenses. On the other hand, the 300 kilograms of cocaine now being loaded on board would sell for $15,000,000 - $50,000 per kilo on the U.S. wholesale market. That represented a gross profit of $7,500,000 over the purchase price in Colombia. It was not all going to Lehder; for this particular flight he was to be paid $3,000 a kilo for transporting the drug - a mere $900,000. Still, you could wreck a few old aeroplanes for that sort of money, and still come out on top. Naturally, the price for Andrew's services would also increase. Naturally.

The cases of cocaine loaded that day, each carefully labeled with the name of its Colombian owner, comprised the very first shipment of the Medellin Cartel. The cartel, under Lehder's guidance, was to become a billion-dollar business and a household name. It was to supply 80 per cent of the avid American market for cocaine, causing untold misery, crime, and death. It was to corrupt and kill politicians, judges and policemen, and send ripples that reached into the 1988 campaign for the White House.

And on that day in January 1978 it all came about because a young British pilot, days short of his 21st birthday, failed to take off with a load of marijuana. No doubt it would have happened anyway. But that is how it began.

*   *   *   *

The Beechcraft, though rugged, was smaller than the Turbo-Commander. It had a legal maximum gross weight of 7,400 lb. What with the 700lb of cocaine, 360 gallons of fuel, the three smugglers themselves, and two Indians put on board to ride shotgun on the precious cargo, it was now seriously overweight. 2,000lb overweight, in fact, which is a suicidal recipe for a small twin-engined aircraft, even with 800 horsepower up front.

Barnes lost his temper and insisted that the two Indians be left behind.

"You can't just keep loading these aeroplanes up and up," he said. "We're heavy enough, without those two goons in the back."

But Lehder refused to tell the Indians to leave. The owners of the cocaine, he said, insisted that it be protected. Their caution was understandable: the history of cocaine smuggling from Colombia is littered with stories of enterprising pilots who have ripped off loads and disappeared. Conversely, it is also littered with the remnants of overloaded aircraft that failed to make it.

Barnes caved in. It was becoming a familiar pattern. "I just wanted to get to hell out of that country," he said later.

And so the Beechcraft took off, or tried to. It was less of a take-off than an accidental departure. Barnes used every ounce of power and every inch of the strip. He reached 90 miles an hour, and still it would not fly. There was the smell of fear in the cockpit as the end of the runway, the jungle, and the ominous wreckage of the DC6 rushed closer.

In desperation, because the only alternative was to crash, Barnes reached down and pulled the lever to retract the undercarriage. In his own words, he "sucked the gear out from under it." And the Beechcraft flew. Just. The stall warning was sounding, the speed refused to increase, and in front of them lay a line of low hills.

"I still remember that takeoff vividly," said Barnes, "because I didn't think we were going to make it. The aeroplane wasn't climbing, the stall warning was on, and the airspeed was the same 90 miles an hour that I had had to jerk it off the ground with. Basically, we flew over that line of hills in ground-effect, on the verge of a stall. We were not flying at all. We were about to crash. But on the other side of those hills was a deep valley. I got over the crest and just stuck the nose right on down, still with full power.

"Everybody started screaming. They thought we were going straight into the ground. But I built my airspeed to 120 knots and all of a sudden that thing started flying. It dug in. If we didn't have that valley there we would have ploughed straight into the ground. We got the aeroplane flying. It dug in. If that valley hadn't been there, we would have ploughed straight into the ground.

"I said to Joe: `I'm not coming down here again. I don't care if we do get busted in Florida now - we almost got killed!' I told him sternly about overloading these aeroplanes, because he kept doing that. It was one of his things. He didn't give a damn about how heavy the aeroplane was."

Andrew Barnes had had the luck of the devil. But the trip was not over. As the overloaded Beechcraft plodded across the Caribbean he struggled to gain altitude, using maximum power to force it above 8,000 feet - the minimum altitude at which to cross Haiti. To take a

38

more direct route, though the Windward Passage between Haiti and Cuba, would have exposed them to detection from the powerful American radar at Guantanamo naval base.   The only alternative would be a long diversion around the eastern tip of Hispaniola, and even with the extra gas tanks in the cabin that might leave them with insufficient fuel to reach Florida.

Which raised another problem: Barnes had forgotten to ask Jack Leibolt how the reserve fuel system worked, and now he discovered that he could not turn it on.   There was plenty of gas, but for all the use it was it might just have well have been sitting in a bowser at Fort Lauderdale.   There was an electric pump, but each time the pilot turned it on the circuit breaker popped out. Finally, in a puff of blue smoke and a very nasty smell, the pump expired altogether.   Nestor Castrion was enlisted to sit on the rubber bladder, in the hope that his weight would force the fuel through to the engines.   It didn't.

While he struggled with this dilemma, Barnes finally reached 9,000 feet with the Beechcraft fishtailing on the outer edge of control.   And then both engines stopped. One moment they were running fine; the next, they simply quit.   Overheating had caused vapour locks in the induction system.   There was no sound in the cramped cockpit but the rush of wind, and the stifled curses of Andrew Barnes as he tried to restart the motors.

The smugglers began a steep glide towards the ocean. They were no more than 2,000 feet from impact when the pilot's frantic efforts succeeded, and the long climb to clear the peaks of Haiti began once more.

Carlos Lehder, who attributed the failure to Barnes' struggle with the reserve fuel tanks, was scared. "Don't touch that bladdle any more," he said. Lehder had a slight speech impediment. It was perhaps his only endearing characteristic.

Without the extra fuel, Barnes reminded him, they were not going to reach De Land and the waiting Larry Greenberger. But Lehder was adamant that he should leave the "bladdle" controls alone. Four narrow escapes from death were enough, even for the reckless Colombian. They therefore agreed on a change of plan: to land on remote Lee Stocking Island in the Bahamas, and to unload the cocaine and the bodyguards.

Lee Stocking Island was virtually uninhabited, but it had a useable airstrip. They would hide the cocaine in the bushes and leave the Indians to look after it while they figured out a way to get it into America.

For once, the new scheme went smoothly. Lehder, Barnes and Castrion took off again and flew fifty miles to Staniel Cay in the Exuma chain, where they were able to telephone an anxious Larry Greenberger.

They also bribed two Bahamian policemen to manhandle the recalcitrant bladder tanks on to the wings in order to fill up the main fuel tanks. There was still insufficient gas to take them back to Lee Stocking Island and on to Florida, so Barnes flew directly to Fort Lauderdale.

He did not, naturally, clear Customs.   He never did. The technique, which worked infallibly, involved flying at wave-top height to the western tip of Grand Bahama Island, then turning left and crossing the Florida coast at Pompano Beach, just north of Fort Lauderdale.   Radar coverage was weak in that area.   Once across the coast, Barnes would   climb to normal traffic-pattern altitude and pretend that he was on a local flight.

Sometimes he would cross Florida and come back from an opposite, innocent direction.   Sometimes he would find an airstrip used for pilot training and join the pattern, practising touch-and-go landings for an hour or so before diverting to his true destination.   It was all intended to confuse the authorities.   And it worked.

Next day, in another aircraft chartered from Charlie Bush - this time a Cessna 210 - Lehder and Barnes returned to Lee Stocking Island and retrieved their cargo of cocaine.

There was no space for the unfortunate Indians, so they were left behind again with the promise that an aircraft would be sent for them next day.   Once more the smugglers penetrated U.S.   airspace without detection, and landed at De Land's grass airstrip where the cocaine was unloaded by Greenberger and his crew into his black Ford Bronco.

Elated, Barnes flew the Cessna back to Fort Lauderdale, buzzing his house at low altitude to announce his return. The trip had been a total success, and it would soon be time to get paid. Sure enough, a few days later, a message came from Carlos Lehder to meet him at a hotel in Orlando.

Andrew Barnes duly flew north, taking with him a friend named Richard Blankenship. Blankenship, who worked for Charlie Bush in a variety of capacities, was staying at the Barnes' house at the time, along with his girlfriend, Cathy Bales. They had been acting as baby-sitters for Barbara while Andrew was away, and when she had to travel in her job as a stewardess for National Airlines.

Blankenship was not an appealing character. Tough and wiry, and immensely strong for a man in his 60's, he affected black suits that made him look exactly like the hood he was. Once upon a time he had been a pilot himself, flying for Allegheny Airlines, but that was before he went to jail for vehicular manslaughter, having killed a child while driving under the influence of alcohol.

When Barnes first met Blankenship the latter was on probation after serving his sentence, working as a "ramp rat" for Charlie Bush, fuelling and washing aircraft, and handling the payroll for the casual labour. Charlie, in fact, was his parole officer. Whether the young

Englishman knew about Blankenship's past when he took him into his home is a moot point, but the two seemed to get on well enough at the time. Well enough, certainly, to sit together in their aircraft on the Orlando runway and count the $100,000 that Carlos Lehder had just handed to Andrew in a brown paper bag.

"I had never seen that much money in my life before," said Barnes. "That was going to get me out of debt. I thought I wouldn't have to fly drugs again. It was not my intention to."

Not all this money was for him. By previous arrangement, $40,000 was to be paid to Charlie Bush for services rendered. But it was still a fair piece of change.

Andrew Barnes had achieved his goal. With one daring mission he had earned enough money to get his ailing transport company out of debt, to retrieve his beleaguered C.46 from Canada (though his wife thought there were better ways to spend the money), and begin to make an honest living again. There would be no more drug flights; of that he was certain.

Well, fairly certain. Well, certainly not cocaine. Even Charlie Bush had been shocked when he heard about the cocaine.

"You shouldn't have done that, Andy," he said.

"I know that, Charlie," replied Barnes. "But you can't tell a guy 'I ain't going to haul that for you' when you're surrounded by twenty guns."

Anyway, it was done now, and he had gotten away free and clear. As the memory of the narrow brushes with death began to mellow into a grand adventure story, to be recounted and embellished round the family barbecue, Barnes began to waver in his resolution not to smuggle cocaine again.

The sums of money were so huge, and the getting of them so quick and easy, that it was tempting to try once more. Just once more. Perhaps just getting out of debt was not enough; he could certainly do with some more working capital. It would be good to be able to buy a spare engine and leave it sitting in the garage. Hell, with that sort of cash he could even forget about the old C.46 and buy another one. In his dreams, dollar signs were flashing in neon lights.

"All of a sudden something happens to you," he told me. "Especially when the guy is asking you to go and do the same thing next week. So I rattled off three in a row, and we had $300,000."

Andrew Barnes was never a drug-user, then or later. But a single exposure had hooked him on an addiction more subtle and more pervasive than cocaine. Overnight, he had become a money-junkie.

* * * *

A few days after the trip to Orlando, Barnes received a message from Lehder, via Charlie Bush. "I'm real proud of you," Carlos said. "You did real good. But there's one problem: we left a suitcase and a box over there on Lee Stocking Island. When you go down to get the two Indians, make sure you bring those two pieces of baggage back."

There was good reason for Lehder's concern: those two "pieces of baggage" contained cocaine with a wholesale value of $1,500,000.

Barnes did as he was told, taking Blankenship with him at the insistence of Charlie Bush. It is not every parole officer who dispatches one of his charges to pick up a load of cocaine from a deserted island. But Charlie had his own rules.

A helper was necessary because Barnes had no wish to stop the plane's engines, in case he had to make a quick getaway, and nor did he want to leave it unattended while they were running. Parking brakes have been known to fail. Nevertheless, he did not want to take Blankenship.

"I didn't like the idea at all," he was to say later. "I didn't like the idea of getting Richard mixed up in this right now. He had just got off probation." But he took him, anyway. Blankenship, he reasoned, was hard up and needed the money to get an apartment of his own. Perhaps he was merely anxious to be rid of a houseguest.

There is some dispute about whether the older man knew the purpose of their trip before they set off. By Blankenship's account, given later in court, Barnes told him he was flying over to collect a bladder tank that had been left behind.

"But I know Andy pretty well," said Blankenship. "He wouldn't go down there strictly for a bladder. A bladder isn't worth that much money.... I'm not that naive. Andy didn't go to Colombia and come back with $100,000 because he brought back flour. I'm a pilot living in the Broward County area. I knew when I left with Andy that we weren't going over to collect a $300 bladder, and spend $600 on the aeroplane going there and back to get it. I knew we were going to get something else."

At all events, they flew together to Lee Stocking Island, landing without incident. The Indian bodyguards had already departed on a passing boat, ignoring instructions to guard the cache with their lives, but they had left the cocaine behind. Barnes sent Blankenship off to look for it, while he sat in the cockpit with the engines running.

"I was going to give him two minutes to dig around back there and see what he could come up with," he said. "And if he couldn't find anything I was going to go and help him. But within a short period of time, Blankenship came running back to the aeroplane with a cardboard box and a duffel bag that we'd left there.

"I said: `that seems to be exactly what Joe said we left behind, so let's not waste any time. Let's get out of here.' But the twin-Bonanza is a rather awkward aeroplane to get up into, and as I was bringing the cargo on board, a golf cart pulled out on to the far end of the runway."

It was a bad moment. The only inhabitant of Lee Stocking Island, who lived in a house nearby, had clearly become irritated by the uninvited traffic on his private airstrip and was coming to make his feelings known. He turned his golf cart on to the runway at the far end and headed steadfastly towards the Beechcraft.

"I told Blankenship, `Let's get to hell out of here,'" said Barnes. "`We don't want to have no confrontation with anybody, let alone with some cocaine on the plane.'"

In the confusion of the moment, with the golf cart and its irate driver heading getting closer by the second, Andrew Barnes forgot about his passenger. "My attention was focused on that golf cart, not really on Blankenship, and I assumed that he was in the aeroplane when he really wasn't. I started pouring the coals to the engines and looked out over there, and he's screaming as he dangles out of the door."

At this point there was not much he could do about it. At maximum power, the Beechcraft roared down the strip as Blankenship struggled to hold on and heave himself into the cockpit. They achieved flying speed just before they reached the golf cart, and Barnes jerked the machine off the runway, almost parting the driver's hair with his wheels.

Blankenship crawled into his seat, but the cabin door proved impossible to close against the suction of the slipstream. They flew all the way back to Orlando with it hanging open.

"Congratulations," said Andrew Barnes to his gasping passenger. "Now you're a smuggler."

The pair reached Orlando via the usual circuitous route, picked up Carlos Lehder and flew him to Fort Lauderdale. Lehder was delighted with the success of the operation, and rewarded Blankenship with $10,000 in cash on the spot. He had, he said, a lot of flying for Andy to do.

* * * *

A few days later, Lehder telephoned Barnes at his Fort Lauderdale home. "Come and take the children to school," he said. It was his code-phrase, used whenever there was a drug shipment ready to move. This time he needed to move the bulk of the first cocaine consignment to the West coast. Barnes took the task without question, picking up the six heavy suitcases from Lehder's apartment and driving them in his van to the airport. For the purpose of the trip he had hired a Piper Aztec from the Opa Locka Flight Centre, assuring them that he was merely taking a passenger to Tallahassee. In fact he intended to take it to Los Angeles via refueling stops at Freeport, Louisiana, and Lubbock, Texas, with six heavy suitcases full of cocaine.

At least, that was the plan.   In the event, the Aztec developed engine trouble after take-off on the last leg of the journey.   The oil temperature gauge on the starboard engine went into the red, oil pressure started dropping, and soon the bearings failed completely.   Barnes had no alternative but to limp back to Lubbock on one engine.

He telephoned Lehder from the airport.   The Colombian, who never did anything by halves, at once chartered a Lear Jet to fly from Los Angeles to pick up the load.

Once again, Barnes was accompanied by Richard Blankenship.   This time he had told the co-pilot what they were carrying.   And indeed, it would have been difficult to pretend otherwise.   The stench of ether in the cramped space of the Aztec's cabin, baking in the heat of the Texas sun,   was overpowering.   Barnes habitually flew with the cockpit windows open, fearful he would suffer ill effects. "I didn't have any idea what cocaine did, or how you could ingest it," he explained later, "but I didn't want to get high just sitting on top of all that stuff."

In spite of this evidence, Blankenship needed to satisfy his curiosity.   He took one of the suitcases into the airport men's room and opened it.   Inside were a number of packages shaped like American footballs, wrapped in heavy plastic.   He hurriedly closed the case and took it back to the tarmac, where Barnes was standing guard over the rest of the consignment.

The pilot was sweating, less from the heat than from the possibility that some sheriff would chance by with a drug- sniffing dog.   "The last thing we wanted to do was to set it down in that part of the country," he said later. "All these border towns are notorious for having narcotics units and drug dogs."

He need not have worried. Lehder duly arrived, and the airport staff was only too happy to help them load 300lb of cocaine, with a wholesale value of $7,500,000, on to the Lear Jet.

No one noticed anything amiss, either there or at Los Angeles. The drugs were through, free and clear.

*   *   *   *

In New York, things went less well.   One of the cocaine-laden suitcases brought from Colombia belonged to Nestor Castrion, who separated it from the main load and traveled north to sell it on the streets of the Big Apple for a potential profit of more than half a million dollars. He showed poor judgment.   Unluckily for Castrion, his talent for smuggling exceeded his marketing research abilities, and his customer for the 26 kilograms of cocaine proved to be an undercover agent for the Drug Enforcement Agency. He was promptly arrested.

Castrion was sentenced to nine years in jail, but served only a few weeks.   He had connections - not with the parole board, but with the Mafia, who staged a dramatic rescue while he was being transferred from one prison to another.   He returned to Miami, while Andrew Barnes flew to Norman's Cay to pick up his wife, Marta, and bring her to Florida to keep him company.   Barnes then flew the couple to California, where Castrion stayed for three or four months and grew a beard.

It seems to have been a successful disguise. For nearly four years, Castrion lived free in Miami under the name of Jamie Sanchez.   He had discarded his wife and married another, also named Marta, who was a Colombian-born American citizen.   And but for an argument with Marta Mark II, he might be living there yet.

However, on one night in 1982, Castrion got drunk and shot Marta in the leg, twice.   He then got into his car, which was his second mistake.   A patrol officer stopped him, he was arrested for drunken driving, and though Marta refused to press charges the police took his fingerprints just the same, and ran them through the computer.

Castrion is now back in a New York jail, serving his nine-year sentence, plus another five for escaping.   "If you're living on the lam, you don't behave like that," said Andrew Barnes piously.

This minor glitch apart, the first Medellin drug run had proved a complete success.   But Carlos Lehder had learned a valuable lesson from the mishaps along the way. He no longer wanted to use other people's dubious aeroplanes, with spatchcocked fuel systems that might deposit cargoes in the Caribbean. From now on there would be an organised operation, with a regular air wing ferrying cocaine from the producers in Colombia to the drug-hungry noses of America.

Lehder had the necessary funds. He had also recruited a crew in California who were willing to accept the hazards of flying in and out of Colombia. What he needed now was someone who could find him a way station in the Bahamas, where his men could stay in safety, and a pilot with an intimate knowledge of the islands who could make the terminal flights into the United States.

He found both in the person of Andrew Richard Barnes.

CHAPTER THREE

The Making of a Smuggler

As I reviewed the transcript of those first interviews, by now running into several hundred pages, it was difficult to reconcile the Andrew Barnes to whom I had been talking with the man whose actions he described in such graphic detail.   Here was a man of 32, highly intelligent, and well able to recognize the consequences and implications of his actions.   A pleasant, courteous, and thoroughly civilised human being.   And yet, as we have just seen, this same man had been prepared to co-operate enthusiastically in one of the most evil conspiracies of modern times - and make no bones about confessing it.   It simply did not fit.

I went back to the tapes, hearing again his calm tones as he described the terrifying incidents that followed his initiation into the drug-smuggling circus.   Amid the contrition, did I sense an element of school-boyish pride in that voice?   A smug satisfaction in having taken on the world and gotten away with it for years?   What made Andrew Barnes tick?   Was it a need for adventure, or nothing more praiseworthy than common greed?   Or was there, perhaps, something in his background or upbringing that turned him on to the crooked path?

Barnes himself has clearly wondered about that.   He likes to claim that he is descended from a long line of blackguards. "Really," he told me, "all my family were Cornish pirates. They all came from Truro. They were lighting up bonfires to lure ships on to the rocks for generations back."

It could be true; the surfacing of ancient genes might account for a lot. But there is certainly nothing in his immediate parentage to suggest that he might take up a life of crime.

He was born in Kuantan, Malaya, on January 14, 1956, just as British rule was coming to an end in the Far East. His father, a former Colonel in the Ghurka regiment, was at this time serving as Superintendent of Police for Kuantan Province, involved in preparing the country for independence. Ironically, in view of the career his son was to pursue, Paul Barnes had the reputation of being a strict and upright police officer; a man with a passion for discipline.

"He was very heavily into law and order," said Andrew Barnes dryly. "My father and I never got along too good, but we have always been civil to each other. Of course, he has taken a pretty dim view of all this, as you can imagine. He's not too thrilled with me getting all messed up like this."

Much of the antipathy between father and son seems to have stemmed from the elder Barnes' detachment from his family, and a somewhat parsimonious nature. One of Andrew's abiding memories is being chided for taking a taxi from the station to his school instead of carrying his suitcase, at the age of eight, for more than a mile.   "My sister has the same opinion of him," he claims.   "He never went out of his way to be friendly to us kids.   He's very good at pinching pennies.   Not exactly miserly, but thrifty.   So I grew up the opposite to that.   I figured I had to make as much money as I could."

His mother, Kay, an attractive, gentle woman, worked as a part-time schoolteacher in Malaya.   The couple had met while she was a nurse on board a hospital ship during the Korean War, and was subsequently married in St. Andrew's Cathedral, Singapore.

Andrew was their second child, preceded by some 18 months by a daughter named Candy.   Initially, brother and sister were educated at the Garden School in Malaya, where their mother taught, but like most families in the Colonial Civil Service, Paul and Kay Barnes sent their children back to school in England at the earliest opportunity.

Thus, at the age of six, Andrew Barnes became a world traveler, spending holidays with his parents in Malaya and the rest of the time at boarding school in England.   His earliest memories are of flying to and fro on a BOAC Comet 4C, stopping in Ceylon, Calcutta, New Delhi, Baghdad, Cairo and Frankfurt.   One day, he told himself, he would be up in the cockpit and flying himself.

The two children were separated when they reached England, though both went to private elementary schools in Exeter, Devon, where an aunt lived.   Candy was placed in Margaret School for Girls; Andy entered the Norwood Preparatory School for Boys, where he was instantly labeled as a "wog", despite his British ancestry. It did not bother him unduly.

He recalled being homesick for the first two terms, but then he settled down to the routine and was happy enough. And the end of each term his aunt would collect the children from school and take them to Heathrow Airport, where they boarded the Comet for Singapore.   It was, in its way, an exotic existence.

The juvenile globetrotting went on for three years, after which the Malayans finally got their country back and Paul Barnes returned to England, a retired police officer.   But like so many former colonial civil servants, he found little to attract him in his own country and small chance of employment.   When a chance to work overseas again presented itself, he seized the opportunity. He became head of security for a chain of gambling casinos at Freeport, Grand Bahama Island.

It made little difference to Andrew and his sister. They merely caught a different flight to join their parents during the school holidays, and flew west instead of east. Andrew grew to know the trans-Atlantic route very well. He flew it 36 times before he left school.

By his own account, he was an average student; not brilliant, but good enough to pass the Common Entrance

Exam and be admitted to Blundell's School at the age of 13, in spite of taking the examination during a bout of influenza. It was an achievement that pleased his father, who had always wanted to attend Blundell's himself.

"I don't think I started out as an inherently bad person," said Barnes reflectively. "At school I never got caned. I had a completely untarnished record in school. I was always considered a sissy, a goody-goody. I participated in everything, but I never did overt things to attract attention to myself or get into trouble. But when I got out of school, without any structure or discipline around me, the whole thing just collapsed. I was out in the wide-open world, and I just went barmy. That's it in a nutshell." Blundell's, founded in 1604, was not Eton or Harrow. But by West Country standards it ranked as a first-class public school. "Public," of course, is the perverse English equivalent of "private" in other parts of the world. Unlike most English schools of its type, Blundell's was no hotbed of snobbery. Most of the 350 pupils were the sons of working men like Paul Barnes, who had saved to give their sons the best education they could afford. Discipline was firm, but fair.

It suited Andrew very well. "It was a good school," he said. "The nice thing about Blundell's, looking back at it, was that it wasn't the snobby type of English public school. It was a down-to-earth school for farmer's boys. Working men who were trying to give their kids a good education sent them there. You didn't see the snobbery.

The teams we used to beat up on and get riled about were the Sherbornes, etc. We got fired up for them."

Cricket and rugby were his games, and he played for the school at both. The latter suited him especially, because of his burgeoning size: "I played loose head prop," he recalled. "We had one of the biggest scrums, and we won all our games. When I was 14 years old I was over 6 foot. I weighed 190 lb. when I left Blundell's. We always had a good rugby team. When we won a big match, even when I was a 15-year-old kid, they would take us to the pub to celebrate on the way home. I guess that's where my love of drinking started."

The one figure that Andrew Barnes remembers from his schooldays is his former housemaster, Christopher Reichwald, for whom he had great respect. "He was a nice guy," said Barnes. "He was 6' 8" tall, and he had won the Military Cross during the war. He was a German teacher, but he was an Oxford blue and a red-white-and-blue Brit. He had half his leg blown off on one side. He was a hell of a man. A very gentle, large man, but his discipline was firm." Reichwald died of cancer in 1984.

The young Barnes also joined Blundell's Combined Cadet Force, which gave him an opportunity to do what he had always hankered after: to fly. Fifteen half-hour trips in the front seat of an aerobatic Chipmunk, cavorting around the sky under the watchful eye of an instructor, were enough to convince Andrew Barnes that this was what he was born to do.

"We used to go to Exeter airport and fly from there," he recalled. "They would take us up the valley and sometimes they would buzz the school. Sometimes we would go over the Exe valley towards Budleigh Salterton, and I was initiated into flying that way. I knew all the theory about flight and I did aerobatics with the instructors. I did about 15 half hour trips. They would let you do everything from takeoff to landing, but they would be riding the controls."

In 1973, his last year at school, he took a course at Hamble with a view to becoming an airline pilot. It was the right move at the wrong time. In that same year, British European Airways and British Overseas Airways merged their operations. Pilots were made redundant by the score, and here was no chance of employment for the young hopefuls at the Hamble training school. But for that merger, the life of Andrew Barnes might have been entirely different, but it did nothing to lessen his determination to fly. He would simply have to choose a different route.

The path that he chose, against his father's wishes, was to leave school and take flight training in Florida. Andrew's academic record was good. He had passed his Ordinary Level examination in 11 subjects and had gone on to take his Advanced Level test at the age of 17 - one year earlier than customary. Again, he had passed in all three subjects. His marks were not great, but he passed.

Paul Barnes wanted his son to stay on at school for another year, to take the exam again to improve his grades, and then progress to a British university. Andrew would have none of it. He had never got on well with his father, and now he was determined to go his own way. Paul Barnes saw the futility of further argument, and surrendered. He agreed to pay his son's tuition at flight school, though that was the limit of his generosity. Beyond that, the boy was on his own. Andrew Barnes now admits that he probably made a mistake: "I think I should have done what my father said and stayed another year there and improved my A-levels, but I took them a year early. He wanted me to improve on everything and grow up a little bit, but I was hell-bent on flying."

At the Burnside Aviation flight-training centre, operating out of the ex-naval airfield at Opa-locka, Miami, Andrew Barnes proved to be an apt pupil. Within six months he had acquired his private and commercial pilot's licenses, complete with multi-engine and instrument ratings. He then became a certified flight instructor, while at the same time getting an associate degree in aeronautical studies from Miami/Dade Community College. He was a natural. And he was still only 17, which made him about the youngest flying instructor in the business.

He was all fixed to go to work, but there was a snag: his application for a green card, permitting him to take employment in the United States, had not yet been granted.   He was limited to flight instructing, at the princely rate of $5 an hour, and whatever odd jobs he could pick up from Burnside Aviation.

Much of his time was spent in delivering new aircraft for the Cessna factory in Wichita, Kansas.   There was no pay involved, only expenses, but young Andrew was not complaining. He was getting a lot of hours in his pilot's log book, and a lot of flying experience.

He was making his way.   It was a boom period for the flight instruction business, with hundreds of former GI's fresh from the war in Vietnam, keen to spend their discharge benefits on learning how to fly.   Burnside Aviation was a thriving concern, with as many as twenty trainees on the downwind leg of the Opa-locka circuit at the same time. Andy had plenty to do.

"It was just crazy," he recalled. "Every year Burnside would trade in their fleet of trainers and send them back to the Cessna factory in Wichita. Those aeroplanes were dismantled and sent to Brazil for re-manufacture, and then sold   as new aircraft. Burnside had such vast quantities of them that they were the only people who had that arrangement with Cessna.   They could keep brand new aeroplanes on the line every year. That's how I got the job. I didn't get paid for it, except expenses, but I loved to just fly all around the country.   I used to find different routes back to Wichita, landing at little towns all around. So I gained a lot of experience from that."

"I was getting paid $5 an hour for instruction work. I was running an apartment in Opa-locka, sharing it with another Englishman, a former London taxi-driver named John Palk, who was doing something similar. So, between sharing the apartment and having a beat-up $100 car, I was making it. Barely making it, but making it. I didn't require any support from home. I became kind of pretty independent."

Andrew Barnes was flying. He was happy. And if only the Immigration Department would come through with his green card, he just knew he could make the grade as an airline pilot.

He also maintained contact with his family, borrowing a small aircraft from the flight line to fly over to Freeport on weekends and holidays. Relations with his father were still strained, but civil.

And then, in 1974, something happened which was to change the course of Andrew Barnes' life: he met Barbara Knaefler.

She was blonde and pert and 21, and a stewardess with National Airlines. She was also the daughter of a wealthy Philadelphia building contractor, who had sent her $1,500 to get her private pilot's license at a time when the airline was on strike. Andrew Barnes just happened to be on duty at the flight school that day. He was assigned to be her flight instructor, and it is arguable that had some other pilot been given the task the whole course of his life would have been changed.

It was some months before Barbara realised that her instructor was three years her junior. With his English accent and obvious education, he seemed far more mature than most young men of her acquaintance. By the time she did learn his age, from a chance sight of his passport, the couple were already in love, and she was pregnant. They were married on February 12, 1976 - Barbara for the second time. The bridegroom was just 20 years old.

From the start, Andrew got along famously with his prospective father-in-law. Lawrence Knaefler had his own aircraft in Pennsylvania, and they could talk the same language. His own father, too, seemed to be mellowing to the idea that he was going to make a career of flying.

Together, Lawrence Knaefler and Paul Barnes put up $25,000 to enable Barbara and Andrew to start their own air transport company. It was called Caribe Air Freight Corporation.

It was not a lot of money with which to start an airline, but it was enough to put down a deposit on a big C.46 cargo aircraft. That C.46 had had a long, hard life.
Built in 1942, it had seen service in World War II before being converted to civilian use, and the engines had not been overhauled for years. It had flown for 28,000 hours when Andrew bought it from Varig Airlines of Brazil for $20,000 down, with a further $45,000 on mortgage.

The repayments of $1,600 per month were the least of the young couple's worries. Hull insurance from Lloyds of London (the only company that would take the risk) cost nearly $10,000 a year, and the cost of maintaining the ancient Pratt and Whitney radial engines was astronomic. They were forever breaking down, and new replacements were unobtainable. Andrew was forced to rely on rebuilt engines, some of which had been overhauled as many as 16 times. Even these cost $30,000 each. There were mechanics to pay, and pilots, too, since Andrew was not yet type-rated on the C.46.

"Most of these guys are dead now," said Barnes, "but they were great old pilots - World War II 'hump' pilots most of them. They had flown that aeroplane over the hump from Burma into China during the war. Real salty old dogs. All heavy drinkers and chain smokers. The salt of the earth."

One of those pilots was Jack Leibolt, the veteran flier who was later to rescue the first Medellin trip from impending disaster. Leibolt was a fascinating character. Trained as an aeronautical engineer in the 1930's, he joined the U.S.A.F. at the outbreak of war and, kept from combat by less than perfect eyesight, became an instructor on a wide variety of aircraft, from the P.47 Thunderbolt to the C.46.

After the war Leibolt flew for Flying Tiger airlines, and then moved on to fly the early corporate jets, but by the time Andrew Barnes found him he was, to quote Barnes, "derelict and a bum in Haiti."

Leibolt was about 55 years old at this point, and had not flown for fifteen years. He was running, in desultory fashion, an outboard motor shop in Port au Prince, and living in a local bar known as "The Snake Pit." The Snake Pit, run by an American named Randy Sanders, was a favourite watering hole for pilots of the drug-smuggling fraternity. Barnes was to become a regular patron. Another resident at this point, in 1976, was Bob Morgan. And it was Morgan, through the ubiquitous Charlie Bush, who alerted Andrew Barnes to the fact that there was an experienced C.46 pilot sitting in Haiti.

Barnes picked up an Air France flight in Miami and flew to Haiti the next day. He told Leibolt his problem. "You've got a *what*?" said Leibolt, looking at the boy with disbelief.

"A C.46. You want to come and fly with me?"

The older man laid down his tools and stood up. "Let's go to work," he said.

It proved a happy partnership. And with Leibolt's help Caribe Air Freight was holding its own. "He really busted his balls for us," said Barnes. "When we had hard times with these engines and stuff, he wouldn't even take any pay."

Andrew Barnes himself was working all the hours God made, drumming up business during the day and flying at night. The C.46 would take off from Miami at 3 a.m., landing in Haiti at first light to load cargo, then taking off for Puerto Rico, or the Dominican Republic, or both. From baseball bats to electronic components, from ladies' underwear to car radios, Caribe Air hauled it across the

Caribbean and back to Florida at the cutthroat rate of twelve and a half cents per pound.

"At one time a pilot in another cargo company swore to God that we had three C.46's," recalled Barnes. "We flew it all over the place. We would do three or four trips a week in that aeroplane."

Competition was fierce. Customers would haggle for the lowest possible price, and then not pay their bills. In addition to everything else, Andrew had to act as his own debt collector. But at least it was all legitimate cargo. They were poor, but they were honest. Barbara was also heavily pregnant and unable to work as a flight attendant.

Andy Jr. was born in July, 1976, but the couple's joy was short-lived. Five days later, just as she got home from the hospital, Barbara Barnes got a message from Philadelphia. Her father had climbed on to the icy roof of a warehouse under construction by his company, and fallen off. He was dead.

The news would have been bad enough at any time; at this juncture it was catastrophic. The engines of the C.46 were beginning to give serious trouble. Had Lawrence Knaefler lived, he might well have helped his son-in-law to finance proper replacements. Relations between the two men were excellent and Knaefler was a rich man, though most of his fortune evaporated in liabilities settled after his sudden death. "I think he had very good lines of credit that he could possibly have extended to us,"

Barbara was to tell me later. "And he was very much behind Andy. My God, he really liked Andy."

But as it was, Andrew was forced to make do with the cheapest second-hand engines he could find, which inevitably broke down in their turn.

"We fell into a bad trap," he said. "We bought cheap engines. We tried to buy two engines for the price of one good overhaul, and those things always eat you up in the end. Flying long distance overseas routes, when one packs up out of your home base it really is a mess. Especially when you've only got one plane."

By now Caribe Air was employing a full-time mechanic to fly on every trip, just in case an engine failed away from base. Which they frequently did. But even that was not sufficient insurance if a breakdown happened while the C.46 was carrying a perishable load. Then the cargo would have to be off-loaded on to another aircraft and paid for, robbing the trip of all profit, and more.

"That happened to us," said Barnes. "We blew an engine over Great Inagua, heading for the Dominican Republic. We had to land in Bimini with a full load on board. We had to transfer it to another company's DC4 to save the guy's load, and by the time we got back it cost us everything. It cost us half another engine to save that guy's load. It was a real mess. If I had it to do again I'd buy another C.46, tear it down and put on two brand new engines, and then buy two more engines and put them in the garage as spares."

In 1976, the point was academic. It was time for a change of direction. Barnes was fond of the old C.46, but the damn thing had become a carnivorous monster with an insatiable appetite for cash. Then he and Leibolt had a bright idea: they would trade it in against a Boeing 707 and move their operational base to Lagos, Nigeria. From there they would ferry Moslem pilgrims to Mecca - it was known as "the Haji run", and it was a lucrative business.

Though the step-up from a World War II cargo plane to a big modern jet sounded extreme, especially for a company in their sort of financial trouble, in fact the difference in value was not great. It was a time when many airlines were replacing their ageing 707's with more profitable Jumbo jets, and there were plenty of 707's, going cheap, lying at airfields around the country. This was especially true the older models with straight-through turbo-jets, as opposed to those that had been re-engined with by-pass fan-jets. The former were quite good enough for Barnes' purpose, and he located one through a Miami aircraft broker, Nigel Winfield.

Winfield was a fellow Englishman. By coincidence, he also came from the West Country town of Exeter, where his father had been a bus driver, and possibly that was why Andrew Barnes trusted him. The consequences were unfortunate.

At first sight, however, the deal seemed perfect. Winfield had a Boeing 707-121 for sale, based in Seattle, Washington. The price was $100,000. He agreed to take the C.46 in part exchange, and to arrange a mortgage for the balance of the purchase price. Barnes and Leibolt already had a contract for the Haji run, and they willingly signed on the dotted line. They set off for Seattle in high good humour to take delivery, leaving the C.46 with Nigel Winfield.

There was one minor snag: neither of them had a type-rating to fly the Boeing. But Leibolt was qualified on the very similar Convair 880, and was confident he would have no difficulty in passing the FAA test. In order to ferry the jet back to Miami they took along another pilot, Dick Wellman, who was to join them in the Haji enterprise.

Though they had bought it sight-unseen, the Boeing did not disappoint them. "It had just come off a travel club lease and had 189 seats," recalled Barnes. "It was the maximum you could put in, single class. That's great for the Haji run. We were just about to load the aeroplane with 15,000 gallons of fuel - we had the cash for that - when this guy calls the sheriff out.

"He said: `Winfield didn't send you out here for this aircraft did he?' We said `yes; here's all the papers.'

"He said: `I'm sorry, those are not worth the paper they're written on.'"

The awful truth dawned. They had been conned.

"We had to scramble back to Miami," said Barnes, "and by the time we got back, our C.46 was gone."

Nigel Winfield, later to be sentenced to life imprisonment on racketeering charges, had sold the C.46 to a Caribbean operator named Charlie Carty, who had taken it to Trinidad. When Barnes and Leibolt tracked him down, he was mildly apologetic. Would they like their aircraft back, or would they rather have $60,000 in cash? Disingenuously, because they wanted to proceed with the deal on the Boeing 707, the two men asked for the money. The check, of course, bounced.

Charlie Carty, too, had been swindled. He had paid $40,000 to Winfield for the C.46, with an agreement to pay instalments on the balance. When Barnes finally got a court order for repossession of the aircraft from the Broward County court, Carty pleaded with the young man to fly it for him so that he could fulfil the commitments he had already taken on. Barnes, broke again, agreed. It was another mistake. When he and Leibolt undertook the first cargo trip to the island of Grand Turk, they discovered that this was where Carty had borrowed the money to buy the C.46, and his creditors were not about to let it escape. They let the air out of the tires and slashed the battery cables.

"It was a real circus," recalled Barnes. "The whole thing went on for a month. We went to the island's British commissioner, and he summoned the Governor who sent the whole regiment out to the airport, armed with rifles. They surrounded the plane, and he said: `I'm going to get to the bottom of this thing.'

"We explained our side. Charlie Carty said we were lying and had stolen the plane from him. The Governor said: `Mr. Carty, the only thing we've ever known you for in these islands is to rip people off and lie.....' It took a night and a day, and then he let us have the plane back."

But that, of course, was before Andrew Barnes acquired a reputation of his own in the islands.

The opportunity to recoup their fortunes on the Haji run had disappeared. It had been a sound idea; ironically, Dick Wellman went on to follow it through and made millions. But Caribe Air Freight was back where it started.

Somehow, against all the odds, the company struggled on. But by the late summer of 1977 the writing was on the wall The C.46 was grounded with mechanical problems for two months after both engines suffered catastrophic failures, and steady customers were disappearing like snowflakes in July.

Without two new engines, or at least two that had had a complete overhaul, Andrew knew that they could not stay in business. He was getting deeper and deeper into debt, and the bank manager was making angry noises.

And so he went to Charlie Bush. Good old Charlie Bush. And Charlie helped him out. To be precise, he paid for one engine, at a cost of $30,000, and arranged a note to pay for the other. It was a generous gesture, or so it seemed at the time.   The old man even offered to find some flying work for Andrew, while his own aircraft was being repaired.

Which was how Andrew Barnes came to meet Vincent Foster, and take his first step outside the law.   But of that, more later.

CHAPTER FOUR

Diamonds Are a Girl's Best Friend

I now knew the mechanics, at least, of Andrew Barnes' rake's progress from innocent English schoolboy to drug smuggler. A combination, by his own account, of commercial misfortune and youthful misjudgment. Would things have been different if he had spent his childhood at home, instead of being dispatched thousands of miles to a boarding school at an age when a boy needs his parents most? Perhaps. I know that he thinks so. But the explanation is too facile to be satisfying. His upbringing, when all is said and done, was no different from that of thousands like him during the hey-day of the British Empire. It was established custom for the children of overseas civil servants to be sent back to England for their education, and though the practice seems psychologically barbaric to some modern eyes, it had its merits. The children were, in a real sense, members of a privileged class. They certainly got a better education than they would have done in the outposts of Empire. And if there are figures to prove that many of them are now in jail as a result, I have never come across such statistics.

No, there had to be something else behind Andrew Barnes' descent into crime, and I was not going to find it without digging more deeply. At this stage Barnes was still free on bail, on his own recognisance, and I arranged to travel to Pennsylvania to meet his wife and family. Perhaps the answer lay there. He had, after all, been married at a very young and impressionable age. Married, moreover, to an older woman accustomed to luxury, who already had one marriage behind her. And if there was one quality that shone through Andrew's character on the evidence so far to hand, it was that of gullibility. He was, perhaps, the most trusting soul I had ever met.

The Barnes' home lay just outside the village of Quakertown, at the end of a long rutted track more suitable for an M1 tank than any more civilised form of transport. It was a modern frame bungalow of no particular distinction, backed by dense woodland but looking out towards open country. The front lawn boasted a large swimming pool, and two fine horses roamed the pasture behind a fence at the far end. Two pick-up trucks, an ancient tractor, and Andrew's faithful Mustang stood on the driveway. There was also a new-looking Thunderbird Turbo-Coupe. This, I was to learn, belonged to his wife.

I was welcomed, if that is the right word, by a scruffy chow dog of moth-eaten appearance and uncertain temper. I skirted it warily, realising from its description that this was the animal that had added to Barnes' troubles a few weeks before by savaging his youngest daughter and putting her in the hospital. Then Andrew emerged, and moments later, I was being introduced to Barbara.

This second series of interviews had been arranged on the pretext that there were inconsistencies in Barnes' original account which needed to be ironed out; details which needed to be added. This was perfectly true, but the real reason behind my visit was to talk to the woman of whom he had given such a glowing description. Andrew's account of his wife and their marriage had been a little too pat, a little too fulsome.

I had asked him during our first session: "How the hell did you manage to keep a marriage intact through all this?"

Andrew had replied: "I don't know. I've got a hell of a wife. She's attractive; she's intelligent. I don't know how I managed to keep the marriage intact, except that it was a very good marriage to start with. She realises that this nonsense has to end."

"But you were in this almost from the moment you got married, weren't you?" I persisted.

"It sounds that way," he admitted. "Of course, there were a lot of times when I wasn't flying. And things were pretty smooth, right up to the time I got popped at Nassau. That's when the last mad scramble was on. Everything else was like going into Washington DC for two days, as far as Barbara was concerned. She never came on a trip with me or anything. She would just see me go off to the airport one day, and show back up three days later."

There was something unreal about this exchange. The spectacle of Barbara Barnes waving good-bye to her husband as if he was going on a shopping expedition, when in fact she knew quite well that he was risking imprisonment or death every time he took off, was bizarre in the extreme.

Such a woman would have to be either stupid or uncaring, or both, and it was immediately obvious that the lady who faced me now across the kitchen table was neither. In contrast to her husband's forced cheerfulness, Barbara Barnes was pinched and harassed, her elegance wilted by anxiety. She was also patently distrustful of my own intrusion in the situation, and had no hesitation in accusing me of trying to reap profit at her expense. Her view was quite simple: this was Andrew's story, and if there was any money to be made, Barbara Barnes wanted it in order to support herself while he was in jail. After all, she said with feminine logic, they had done the smuggling, so they should get the reward.

It was not a promising beginning. A long and futile argument ensued about the "Son of Sam" laws (which prohibited convicted felons from profiting from their activities), plus lengthy explanations of the slim prospects of rich pickings in Hollywood. At last, to my intense relief, she agreed to answer my questions.

How had she felt, I asked, when Andrew handed her that very first envelope of cash from Carlos Lehder?

"I had never seen $5,000 in cash before," she replied. "I was scared, of course. I didn't really understand why he would want to do something like this. But at the same time I didn't think marijuana was that bad a thing, so in my mind it wasn't immoral. He was breaking the law, but it was kind of adventurous, really. Of course I was scared and I didn't like it, but we didn't have any money; we had a little baby; we were absolutely flat broke."

That made one thing clear: Barbara Barnes had known exactly what her husband was getting into. She had raised no objection.

And of course, as I reminded her, the $5,000 had been swiftly followed by a much greater sum - payment for the first Medellin shipment of cocaine. How had she felt when that landed on her doorstep? "Wonderful," said Barbara Barnes. And she laughed. "I did. I really did."

"Presumably he told you where that money was coming from?" I asked. "He didn't pretend he found it under a stone?"

"No," she said. "But at that point there was no mention of cocaine. I thought it was still marijuana. I don't think it was until later that I actually knew what it was."

"I had promised her a diamond ring and a Mercedes Benz," interjected Andrew, and a small bell rang inside my brain.

"Tell me more about that," I said.

Spasmodically, the story began to come out. The couple disagreed on points of detail, with Barbara seeking to minimize her own responsibility, but the thrust of the tale was plain enough. At that time, in late 1977, their marriage was not going well. There had been terrible rows, mostly over Andy's insistence that she should give up her $12,000 a year job as a flight attendant with a major airline. Barbara had worked before and after their marriage, and had returned to flying soon after their son Andy Jr. was born.

Now the baby was three months old, and Andy found himself having to stay at home and care for him while his wife went off for days at a time. He didn't like it. She insisted that they needed the money in order to survive.

"He wanted me to quit my job so badly," she told me. "He just couldn't understand how I could keep working. I said, 'but we don't have any money. I have to.' There was no other choice."

It was an impasse. Andy would not leave the subject alone; she would not yield. And then, in the course of one violent verbal conflagration, Barbara Barnes said something she was to come to regret.

"Buy me a house and a diamond ring," she said, "and then I'll quit my job."

"And a Mercedes too, I suppose?" retorted Andy.

"Yeah, a Mercedes, too."

That row took place six months before Andrew Barnes met Carlos Lehder. Barbara claimed during our interview that she never meant it; that she only made the demand to put the subject to rest.

"I figured he would drop it," she said. "I would never get these things. I figured if I made these demands I wouldn't get any more harassment about quitting this job." She was wrong on all counts.

Andrew Barnes had not forgotten. Shortly after the first payment from Lehder he arrived home with a diamond ring and the deeds to a luxurious house in Coral Springs. And a Mercedes. For good measure, to prove he was no cheapskate, he gave his wife a pair of diamond earrings and a grand piano. His creditors could wait. What the hell - there was plenty more where that came from.

"Now will you quit that damned job?" he said triumphantly.

Barbara Barnes knew when she was beaten. "I got held to my word," she told me ruefully. And so she took the goodies, and she quit her job.

"I never wanted anything," she insisted. "I would have been happy without those things. That was what he didn't understand. I was happy with him, with my little baby, and with my job. To me, I had a wonderful life."

Nevertheless, nothing went back to the store. Barbara Barnes played the Shakespearean maid: she said 'no' - and took it.

"But how did this work on your conscience?" I asked her. "Did you feel you were in any way responsible for pressuring Andy to go into this business."

"No," she said.

"She never pressured me at all," chipped in Andrew loyally. "It was my pressure on her. She never demanded any of those things."

"I never wanted anything," Barbara insisted. "I was happy with my job."

But later that day, as we sat alone in my car on our way to get some beer from the local pub, Andrew had second thoughts. "You know," he said, "I'm prepared to take the blame for what I've done. All of it. But maybe, now I come to think about it, Barbara does have some responsibility."

For it transpired that after that monumental row, and long before the appearance of Carlos Lehder, Andrew Barnes had made not one but two unsuccessful attempts to enter the world of drug smuggling and get the cash he needed so badly. I started my tape recorder and began to learn about Vincent Foster.

CHAPTER FIVE

The Suing of a Samaritan

Vincent Foster and his friend Princeton Harris, a Fort Lauderdale pimp, were Jamaicans. They were regular customers of Charlie Bush, frequently renting small aircraft to fly to the Bahamas, and Andrew saw nothing wrong in acting as their pilot and earning a few dollars. Foster, who knew the Englishman's financial situation perfectly well, asked him if he would like to earn a few more. He needed to go to Andros, he said, to pick up some lobsters.

Andrew Barnes was young and naive, but he was not stupid. No one in his right mind was going to pay all that money to collect a few shell-fish; besides which, they were to land at a small airstrip on the northern end of the island instead of the main Andros airport, and he had specific instructions not to clear customs. He guessed that the cargo would be marijuana. He was right.

Flying a single-engined Cessna belonging to Charlie Bush, they landed without incident. Foster, who was using the alias of Zim Roy Green, left Barnes at a nearby hotel while he went into town with a group of Bahamians to negotiate the purchase.

He returned smiling broadly. It was all fixed, he said. The cargo would be delivered after dark, at ten o'clock that night. All Andrew had to do was to taxi to the far end of the runway, where a road passed close by, and it would be waiting for them.

It was so simple. Barnes did as he was told. Sitting in the unlit aircraft, the engine ticking over smoothly, the two men waited in the steamy dark. A car approached from the direction of the town, flashed its lights, and stopped. Foster began to climb out.

"Be careful of that propeller," shouted Barnes. "I'm going to leave the engine running."

"Do that," came the reply. "We might need to get out of here in a hurry if these bastards try to rip me off."

Foster, in fact, had a very good reason for a quick departure: the bundle of money with which he intended to pay for the marijuana had $20 notes on the outside, but was otherwise stuffed with $1 bills. He had no wish to be around when the Bahamians counted it.

Just to make sure, Foster insisted that the three bulging suitcases should be brought to the aircraft before he paid. Grumbling but unsuspicious, the Bahamians did as he asked. Barnes unstrapped himself and went to the rear cabin to make sure that the load was stowed securely.

It was then that he heard the scream. Within seconds the Bahamians were at the door of the aircraft, demanding their marijuana back.

"I thought they'd shot him or something, and were ripping him off," Barnes told me. "I said, 'Go on, take the stuff. Get the hell out of here.'"

The Bahamians took their suitcases and vanished into the night, their cars throwing up plumes of dust as they accelerated away as fast as they could.   Andrew Barnes was left by himself with an illicit aircraft, a briefcase full of money, and a body on the runway.   Things had definitely taken a turn for the worse.

Heart pounding, he switched off the engine and took his flashlight to see what had happened.   One glance was enough.   Vincent Foster had walked into the spinning propeller.   His head was split almost in half, as though struck by a hatchet.   One leg was virtually severed, ragged ends of tendons protruding from the kneecap. And from a gash in his stomach that made Andrew sick to look at, grey loops of intestine were bulging obscenely. There was blood everywhere.   Not unreasonably, Barnes decided that his passenger was dead.

The runway stretched ahead of him invitingly.   He could climb back in the cockpit, open the throttle, and be away in a matter of seconds.   The aircraft seemed to have suffered no vital damage: the propeller was slightly bent, but serviceable.   There were no witnesses; at least, none likely to talk.   If he got the hell out of Andros right now, no one would be any the wiser.   It was the sensible thing to do.

It was not, however, the sort of behaviour expected of an English public schoolboy.   Expediency wrestled with his conscience, and conscience won in two straight falls. Uncaring that his decision would quite likely land him in jail, Andrew left the body where it lay and taxied the Cessna towards the small airport hotel to look for help.

Fortunately the hotel bar was still open for business. The police were summoned; a doctor was called. Ten minutes later Barnes was back in the cockpit with a Cuban physician beside him, heading back down the runway to find the corpse of Vincent Foster, a police car on his tail. For the novice drug smuggler, it was not the most auspicious start to a life of crime.

As it turned out, Foster was not dead. He was still breathing, though unconscious, when the doctor reached him. While the police left to fetch emergency supplies of blood and medical equipment, the Cuban set to work to sew up the gaping holes in the Jamaican. When he ran out of sterile sutures, he used fishing line instead. And when he was sure that nothing was going to fall off or fall out, he persuaded Andrew to fly himself and his patient to Nassau and the nearest hospital.

The policeman came, too. He had some questions to ask Andrew Barnes.

Luckily there was no trace of drugs on board the Cessna, nor any guns. Barnes spun an unlikely story, claiming that they had been about to take off for Fort Lauderdale when his passenger, who had come in a taxi, remembered he had left his briefcase behind. Foster, he said, had got out to recover the case, and had walked into the propeller.

The policeman watched the ambulance drive away and laid an almost affectionate hand on Andrew's arm. He knew bullshit when he heard it. "We are going to have to fill out a report on this," he said. "I don't believe any of that jive-ass stuff."

It was now one o'clock in the morning. Barnes had left the Cessna right outside the Nassau main terminal building, where the regular Air Bahama flight would be arriving in a few hours. "Just let me go and park the 'plane," he said casually. "Then I'll answer any questions you want."

The Bahamian constable made his one mistake. "Okay," he said, "go and park it."

Back in the pilot's seat, Barnes did some quick thinking as he started the engine and watched the instruments climb into the green. He had plenty of fuel, and no particular wish to spend the night in Nassau. Especially since, from the way things were shaping up, the accommodation might be uncomfortable.

In the control tower, a bored duty officer watched with astonishment as the little Cessna roared across the tarmac of the parking ramp and shot into the sky. He snatched up his microphone to shout a protest - to order the fugitive to return. But Andrew had not switched on his radio - and would not have answered if he had. He was free and clear, and headed for home.

"I had to fly an instrument flight plan to get back, so I just radioed it in to Miami Centre," he recalled. "You are not supposed to do it, but I came up with some cockamamie story that I was leaving out of Rock Sound, Exuma.   Back then you could get away with murder. Now, if you tried something like that, you'd be surrounded by D.E.A. helicopters when you got to Lauderdale.   But I was an instructor back then.   I knew every way in and out of the Bahamas and the U.S."

Sure enough, there were no drug enforcement agents waiting for him at Fort Lauderdale.   In fact there was no one at all.   Barnes parked the bloodstained Cessna on Charlie Bush's ramp and climbed a 12-foot security fence to get out of the airport.   He telephoned Barbara to come and pick him up.

"Get out of here, quick," he said.   "Zimmer's dead." Barbara, who had no idea what her new husband had been up to, dutifully drove him home.   He seemed, she said, upset.

Vincent Foster did not die; a fact which was to cause Andrew Barnes no little inconvenience.   By great good fortune an English brain surgeon was holidaying on Nassau that week, and his expert treatment saved the drug dealer's life.

Foster showed his gratitude by neglecting to pay his hospital bill, and then proceeding to sue Barnes, without whose help he would certainly have died, for five million dollars.   He alleged negligence on the part of the pilot, and the case rumbled on for five years before being finally settled out of court.   Never once in all that time was the purpose of Foster's presence on Andros mentioned.

All in all, it had been an expensive lesson on the perils of the drug trade. And, for that matter, on the dangers of misplaced chivalry. But Andrew Barnes, still wet behind the ears, had yet to learn that when you lie down with dogs you get up with fleas. Nor, for that matter, would he ever learn.

* * * *

Undaunted by his disastrous first foray into airborne smuggling, he tried again. It seemed to be the only thing to do: the C.46 was still grounded, creditors were beginning to circle his wagon like an Indian war party, and there was still the unresolved question of Barbara's job and her conditions for leaving it. This time the man behind the deal was Bob Morgan. The introduction, once again, came from Charlie Bush.

Bush and Morgan had known each other since 1974, when Charlie's son was lost while flying a twin-engined Beechcraft over the Caribbean. Morgan, who was operating a couple of Beechcraft out of Haiti in a reasonably legitimate operation at that time, joined in the search. "Charlie always felt indebted to Morgan," said Barnes, "because they were out there ploughing around 12 hours a day, flying a hundred feet off the deck to look for his son."

The chance to repay the debt came some months later, when Morgan was suddenly expelled from Haiti. Given the reputation of the place, this was quite an achievement in itself, but the circumstances were exceptional.

With ten passengers on board, Morgan was landing one of his twin-engined Beechcraft at Port au Prince when it was hit by a sudden downdraught. The phenomenon is not unusual at this particular airport, which is flanked by mountains rising to 12,000 feet. In the late afternoon, cool air frequently cascades down the slopes. Caught on final approach, Morgan applied full power, but the aircraft refused to climb. It crashed on to a road beside the runway, striking a school bus and ending on its back.

Luckily, only one passenger was injured in the crash, suffering a broken arm. Unluckily, that passenger happened to be the son of a Haitian cabinet minister. There was an inquiry, and, to the minister's rage, Morgan was found not to have a valid pilot's license. He was promptly deported.

His aircraft, however, were not confiscated. Morgan took them to Fort Lauderdale, to Bush Aviation, and called in the debt. He was given parking space, a workshop and a hangar. Plus invaluable access to Charlie's contacts.

Bob Morgan was one of the more interesting characters among the drug-smuggling fraternity. In addition to owning a fleet of eight DC 3's, which he used mainly to bring marijuana into Georgia, he was also the joint proprietor of R.P.B. Industries in Florida, which manufactured Ingram Mac-10 submachine guns. He had bought the arms manufacturing company, in partnership with Jack Leibolt, from his drug-smuggling profits.

Morgan was already a convicted felon at the time. In his youth, spent as a poor white in Georgia, he had been jailed for changing the serial numbers on stolen radios. This fact prevented him from legally possessing a firearm but not, apparently, from making them. Since the Mac-10 was to become the weapon of choice for most smugglers and street dealers, the deal showed considerable foresight and business acumen.

Alas for Bob Morgan, however, he was destined to start a 30-year prison sentence in 1980, after being caught unloading 5,500 lb. of marijuana from a DC 3 in Labelle, Florida, and never really enjoyed the profits of his diversification. He transferred his interest in the company to Jack Leibolt, who subsequently sold it for several million dollars and retired on the proceeds.

But that was to come. Now, in October 1977, business was thriving. He and Leibolt approached Andrew Barnes with an offer: would he like to earn some money? In the circumstances it was a rhetorical question. Said Barnes: "I was so strapped for cash I would do anything right then, and he offered me a job to fly his DC 3 to Colombia to pick up some pot. I was going to get $30,000 for it. Something lke that. I was hare-brained enough, broke enough, and desperate enough to try it."

It seemed like no big deal.   "In Florida at that time," he explained,   "a lot of people were running drugs to shore up failing enterprises.   The money is so easy that you never think about complications like getting caught, or crashing. You think: it was so easy to get that $100,000 in a briefcase, it will be just as easy next month to get another hundred.   But it's not, of course.   So the money goes, time's gone by, you're losing valuable time and you're losing your reputation.

"And once you realise that your reputation is shot - the first time you get thrown in jail - and your pride is gone - you come out, and it's a lot easier.   I guess it's like a hooker on the street.   She hates selling her body the first three or four times, but it only takes the first time she gets thrown in jail and her whole attitude changes.   She's an old pro.   The curtain comes down and it's `What the hell. I don't care.'   That's the way it is when you start living a life of crime.   And I guess it is living a life of crime.   You don't think of it that way until somebody says: 'hey man, you're a criminal.'   It really is like that.   It's insidious.   It sneaks up on you."

"We were all naive," he admitted.   "We thought that smuggling a little pot to save your airline might not be acceptable, but you could live with it."

"It was kind of noble," added Barbara.

Andrew: "None of us wanted to haul cocaine. There is a big difference between hauling cocaine and pot."

Barbara: "The way it happened was like it was kind of simple and basic, and then it turned into this big thing.

Andrew: "We started off in the amateur leagues, and all of a sudden it turned into a horrible nightmare with this coke."

For the moment, however, Bob Morgan's proposition did not involve cocaine. But it was not an amateur operation either. In fact the proposed scheme was slightly more complex than most. There would be two aircraft involved. Morgan and his stepbrother, James Addison, would fly a twin-engined Beechcraft to Port au Prince, Haiti, where they would wait until the DC 3, flown by Barnes and Jack Leibolt, returned from Colombia.

At first, everything went well. The DC 3, with 7,500 lb. of marijuana in the cabin, landed at Port au Prince on schedule. There was no problem with the customs authorities - they had been well paid by Morgan to look the other way. Then the two aircraft changed co-pilots and took off together, flying wingtip to wingtip towards Florida. The idea was that if they were spotted by radar, the two planes would only appear as a single blip on the screen. The authorities, they hoped, would then be quite happy when one aircraft cleared through customs at Fort Lauderdale. And it worked, exactly according to plan.

Morgan and Leibolt made a normal approach to the airport, their Beechcraft as clean as a hound's tooth, while Barnes and Addison dived for the deck and sneaked in through his favourite radar gap at Pompano Beach. They then flew round the Everglades and turned back, as though they had come from Fort Myers. Their phoney flight plan alleged that the flight had originated from an uncontrolled mosquito-spraying airstrip in the area.

This time, Barnes thought he had it made. The air traffic controllers in Fort Lauderdale tower displayed no suspicion, and he and Addison parked the laden DC 3 on Charlie Bush's ramp. Their part of the operation was over. It only remained for the unloading crew to take off the marijuana and spirit it away. But when it came to going awry, the best laid plans of mice and men had nothing on the illicit schemes of Andrew Barnes.

The common sense thing to do would have been to go home, lie low, and wait for payment. But common sense and Andrew Barnes were perfect strangers. He had to see what was happening, to see how the unloading crew coped with their end of the operation in such a public spot. Half an hour later he returned to Bush Aviation, with Barbara driving the van and little Andy on his lap.

The scene was total commotion. The DC 3 was surrounded by police cars, their lights frantically flashing, and sad-looking men were being led away in handcuffs. Someone had talked. Barbara stamped on the brakes and turned round in a hurry. Not fast enough: they were stopped by the police.   Barnes was convinced he was about to be arrested.

"What are you doing here?" asked the motorcycle patrolman. He was hardly to know that the big man in the van, dangling a baby on his lap, was actually the pilot of the marijuana-laden DC 3.   If the suspicion crossed his mind, he must have reasoned that nobody could be that stupid.

Barnes dredged his mind for a reasonable explanation. "We're trying to find U.S. 1," he said feebly.   "We got lost and turned into the airport by mistake."

The policeman accepted the lie without question. That sure was a cute kid they had there.   "Follow me," he said. "You guys don't look like you could be doing anything." He started his machine and guided them out through the chaos.   Barnes and his wife breathed heartfelt sighs of relief.

In the event, the only people who fell into the net were the unloading crew, and Bob Morgan's stepbrother - who had hired them.

Addison was unlucky.   Like Barnes, he too had returned the airport, but he had delayed his arrival until a time when the unloading crew should have finished their job and departed.   They were still there, and in handcuffs, because Bob Morgan had given them a van with a dead battery with which to do the job.   It refused to start, and they were caught red-handed.

As for Addison, stopped by the police, he lacked the protective coloration of a baby on his lap. His driver's license and social security card were demanded, and it was quickly found that he was wanted for escaping from a work-release program in Alabama. But for that, the police might never have discovered that one of the two sets of fingerprints all over the cockpit of the DC 3 belonged to him.

It would be years before they realised that the others belonged to Andrew Barnes, for Addison kept his mouth shut. He admitted ownership of the aircraft, but claimed it had been reported stolen the day before. This was perfectly true. Most aircraft used for drug smuggling are reported stolen after they have taken off. Just in case. Others are leased by their real owners to fictitious offshore companies, so that all responsibility can be disclaimed if they are caught.

Morgan had done both. He managed to pretend no connection with the smuggling operation. Nevertheless he lost the aircraft, confiscated by customs. James Addison went to prison for six months on the escape charge. Andrew Barnes was never even questioned. Nor did he get paid.

Charlie Bush, meanwhile, was not best pleased. Why the hell did Barnes have to park a plane-load of marijuana right on his doorstep, he demanded to know? But having already talked his way out of this mild embarrassment, Charlie's annoyance was mainly synthetic.   For he now knew beyond doubt that Andrew Barnes was willing to do almost anything for money, and he had plans for the young pilot.

Out of the goodness of his heart, the C.46 was re-engined and dispatched to Canada where, Charlie said, friends of his would keep it safe from the greedy fingers of repossession crews.   When Andrew returned there would be things to do and people to see.

People like Carlos Lehder.

CHAPTER SIX

An Island Called Norman

In April 1978, the Immigration Department finally gave Andrew Barnes the Green Card for which he had waited so long; the precious permit enabling him to work for an American employer. The trouble was, he no longer needed it. The bureaucrats were a little late. The man to whom they were granting this cherished privilege was not the ambitious, clean-cut young Britisher who had applied for it. Andrew Barnes was by now a fully-fledged professional drug smuggler, a vital arm of the Medellin Cartel, who had already committed enough crimes to put him behind bars for years. But they gave him a Green Card, just the same. Barnes never used it.

Had the card come through six months earlier the whole story of his life might have been different. He could, and probably would, have abandoned his failing business and gone to work for an airline. Alternatively, if Caribe Air Freight had by some miracle recovered, he could have drawn the salary from which he had hitherto been barred by federal regulations. But none of this happened. He was in too deep; making too much money; enjoying himself too much. For Andrew Barnes, his newly legitimised status was little more than a sick joke.

He has the Green Card still. It is not much use to him now.

By their own account, neither Andrew nor Barbara Barnes saw themselves as criminals in those early days. Cocaine, if they thought about it at all, was merely a fashionable vice of the rich and famous. There was even a romantic aura to their smuggling activities, a swashbuckling camaraderie among the brethren of the coast. It was a gentleman's occupation, in an odd sort of way.

"Nobody got hurt," said Barbara reminiscently. "Everybody did what they said they were going to do. Everybody got paid, and everybody went away happy. It was like a great pirating adventure, like hundreds of years ago. It was so different. Everybody had families and kids and was trying to make a business go."

There was, apparently, a terrifying normality about the whole affair. In the afternoons, while Barnes and his crew were preparing their aircraft for a long night flight into Colombia, the families would picnic under the wings, drinking beer and Coke. Everyone knew exactly what was going on. Nobody cared.

Social evenings at the Barnes home were like those of any other yuppie couple (Barnes being upwardly mobile in the most literal sense). "Leibolt and Morgan used to come over to dinner," Barbara recalled. "Leibolt would make sukiyaki. He set our kitchen on fire one night with banana flambé, using over-proof rum. He set his moustache on fire.

"It used to be fun. It's hard to describe. Now, it's like an evil, dirty thing, because people are getting killed. They're ripping each other off. It was a whole different era. It was like it was too good to be true, and I guess it was."

Andrew Barnes certainly no longer sees himself as a glamorous character. "I'm a twat," he told me candidly. "The net result of all those years of carrying on like that is that I'm going to be getting out of this mess at 35 or something, with a bad reputation, kind of having squandered the last 15 years of my life.

"I'm not suggesting for a moment that I'm not a menace to society. I regarded myself as a menace to society at the time. But I've come forward, and decided that those days in my life are finished with. I'm never going to touch the controls of another aeroplane to head south to Colombia.

"I shall lose my licenses, anyway. That's part of the deal. I view myself as somebody who will do some jail time, and who should do some jail time. I've got some problems I need to work out. But I'm looking to get out of this thing - not to slide out of it, but to seal this chapter of my life with a full stop, and start a whole new chapter. I think I can do that. Maybe I'm being over-optimistic."

But how would he feel, I asked him, if he discovered that his son Andrew had become addicted to the cocaine he smuggled, like so many other American youngsters?

"Well, that's it," replied Barnes.   "I would be devastated.   Absolutely.   The thing that eludes all of us smugglers is that it starts off like a financial necessity.   It started with me that way.   I didn't even know what cocaine was, except that I had heard about it.   That first time I said I didn't want to haul coke, because I'd heard that you got a lot more punishment if you were caught with coke.   That it had more effect on people.   Now, as a result of what we've done, there are things like crack houses, and stuff like that.   It's lowered the value of the drug to the point where they are selling it in ten-dollar bags.   I think Lehder understood.   He had the game plan on it.   He had the overall view of doing this thing.   But people like me - and I think it was true of a lot of the pilots - they look at it as a means to an end to try to make a buck.   They don't look at it as some grand scheme to screw up the fabric of American society, that it is becoming.   You don't look at it that way.   You look at it as taking a risk, a one-time risk you think, to make some money to get your life straightened out.

"But of course it isn't that way at all.   It winds up like getting into a whirlpool.   It turns slow and easy at the top, but you still can't quite get out of it.   You are swimming, but it is still easy and slow.   It kind of puts you to sleep and numbs you.

"But it's at the virulent bottom where it starts whipping you round and spits you right out as a piece of garbage.   You have to go all the way down to the bottom and get spat back out before you can start again. There is no way you can stop that whirlpool in the middle, and your whole life just disintegrates into that chaos."

It was a pretty speech, and very possibly sincere. Barbara Barnes is made of sterner stuff. Unlike her husband, willing to turn on remorse at the flick of a probing question, there was little sense of penitence about her that day. Merely a regret for good times gone, and for a fortune squandered; for a lost house beside the golf course in Coral Springs, and for a Mercedes Benz that no longer sits in the garage.

She said of Andrew: "He gives everything away. If somebody needs something, he gives it to them. I've been on his case about that for years. I wouldn't mind if he gave it away after everything had been taken care of, but he gives it away and then we're sitting here saying, 'hey'?"

"If you had wanted to, could you have stopped him at the outset?" I asked. Barbara affected to give the point serious consideration.

"You have to know Andy, and our relationship," she said. "If I object to something he'll be sure to do it. So there was no point in my arguing with him about it."

But then, I already knew the answer to that question. Barbara Barnes had told me how she felt when Andrew brought home the proceeds of that first cocaine-smuggling expedition.

"Wonderful," she had said. "I really did."

It was hardly the voice of disapproval.

* * * *

In the spring of 1978, there was not long to wait before Barbara Barnes could feel wonderful all over again. With his first load of cocaine distributed, and money in his pocket, Carlos Lehder was ready to begin his grand design. He would set out to subvert American society by satisfying its craving for narcotic drugs, and make millions in the process. Whether this ambition was inspired by politics, or as an act of revenge for putting him in prison some years before (he had been convicted of smuggling marijuana in the cylinders of imported aircraft engines) is unclear. His skill and determination to carry it out, however, were all too plain.

Lehder had already selected a base for his operations, with the advice of Andrew Barnes. It was Norman's Cay, a tiny island in the Exuma chain, some 75 miles south east of Nassau. Norman's Cay was ideal for the purpose. It had an airstrip, about ten houses, and an hotel with a few associated chalets that was owned by a Canadian. There was also a small yachting marina. The tiny indigenous population all worked for the hotel, and were thus easily controlled once the establishment had been bought.

Brandishing large quantities of cash, the Colombian had little difficulty in taking over Norman's Cay, though a few of the residents did hold out for a while. Technically, however, the island itself was the property of the Bahamian government.   Again, no problem - not to a man like Carlos Lehder.

Andrew Barnes flew to Nassau with two large suitcases containing three and a half million dollars, which he handed to a Bahamian lawyer named Nigel Bowe.   Bowe, known locally as "Bagman Bowe" for his role in transactions between the smugglers and Bahamian Prime Minister Sir Lynden Pindling, saw that the money got to its proper destination. It bought Lehder the parcel of land containing the yacht club, hotel and airstrip.   He would have to winkle out the local residents one by one. Basically he now had his own private island, to do with as he pleased.

All this, however, took a little time.   Before the deal was completed, Lehder had another job for Andrew Barnes.   He was to take a newly purchased Beechcraft Queen Air down to Pine Cay in the Turks and Caicos Islands, and there meet a cocaine shipment being brought in by Jack Carlton-Reed and Russ O'Hara from Colombia.

Carlton-Reed was a convicted drug smuggler who had once made his living flying marijuana from Mexico into Arizona and southern California.   But he had served his time   and retired from the game.   When Lehder found him he was earning an honest living as, of all things, a cook in Reno, Nevada.   He even hated flying; it terrified him.   It was Lehder's promise of abundant money that overcame his fear.

The two men were to work together for several years, eventually to be tried and sentenced together. They had something in common: both enjoyed smoking pot and snorting cocaine.

Russ O'Hara was a very different character; the son of a preacher. He was working for a radio station in California at the time of his enlistment, having entered the entertainment business in the early 1960's after two years in college.

O'Hara, whose real name was Eugene Nealeigh, was not a complete beginner. Together with a man named John Finley Robinson, who also worked in radio, he had smuggled two or three loads of marijuana into the U.S. from Mexico prior to 1978, but he hardly ranked as a hardened professional.

"He was just a disillusioned disk jockey with a private pilot's license, looking for something that wasn't there," Barnes told me.   "He wasn't a bad little pilot. He was a wild and crazy guy; a lot of fun."

Now, having co-operated with the police, O'Hara is working as a disk jockey again. He was never charged with any offence.   Robinson, who later joined him on flights to Colombia, was also lucky and escaped with probation.

Barnes knew Pine Cay well. It lay among the Caicos Islands, to the south east of the Bahamas chain, and had once been notorious as the headquarters of the ruthless women pirates, Anne Bonney and Mary Read. It was not an inappropriate site for what Barnes intended to do.

In his legitimate flying days he had often called there, carrying groceries and generator parts for the owner of the 12-room island hotel, the Meridian Club. There would be no problem, he thought. The place was remote and practically uninhabited, and he rated the hotelier, American Bill Coles, as a friend.

The rendezvous with Carlton-Reed's Piper Navajo was set for early morning. Barnes flew down the day before, staying at the Meridian Club and spending a pleasant evening chatting to Coles. He did not, of course, tell him the purpose of his visit. In the morning, the hospitable Coles insisted on accompanying him to the airstrip, which he owned.

Barnes cursed under his breath. "There's no need to hang around, Bill," he said. "I'm just going to check this engine out."

The Queen Air was brand-new. There was nothing the matter with the engine. Barnes opened the cowling and pretended to search for a non-existent oil leak as the time for his rendezvous approached. And still the friendly American would not leave.

Devoid of further excuses, Barnes fastened up the cowling and stood beside the aircraft.

"What are you waiting for?" asked Coles.

"You'll see in a moment," replied Barnes grimly.

Minutes later the Navajo swooped in for a landing, rolling up to park beside the Queen Air. Without a word, ignoring the hotelier, Carlton-Reed and O'Hara began moving heavy suitcases full of cocaine from one aircraft to the other.

Two Colombians, a young man and a teenage girl, were also transferred. They were illegal aliens who Barnes had agreed to smuggle into the U.S. along with the drugs. He was nothing if not versatile.

Coles' jaw dropped. "This looks like some sort of safari to me," he said. "You'll be hearing about this." He drove off to the hotel and, Barnes was uncomfortably aware, a telephone that would connect him with U.S. Customs.

But there was nothing for it. Barnes had to take off and go somewhere. He was now flying, in his own parlance, "a hot buggy." The tail numbers on the Queen Air would have been transmitted to every control tower in Florida, and even if he made his usual undetected entrance into U.S. airspace, the police would be like gnats round a bug-zapper almost as soon as he rolled to a halt.

He might, if he was lucky, escape arrest. But the cocaine would be lost, and so would the aircraft. As would his prospective earnings of $100,000. Barnes regarded Carlos Lehder as a generous man. But he suspected that he was not that generous.

The original plan had been for Andrew to rendezvous with his unloading crew, led by Richard Blankenship, at Orlando airport.   Orlando, he now realised, would be much too public.   He might as well try to land his illicit cargo on the White House lawn.   Consulting his maps and his memory, Barnes dived down as low as he dared, salt spray clouding his windshield, and slithered beneath the probing fingers of coastal radar.   He had decided to sneak into Winter Haven, a private airfield with an excellent runway, fifty miles south west of Orlando.

There was no control tower at Winter Haven; no nosy officials.   He simply landed, parked the Queen Air and $17,000,000 worth of cocaine in a line of innocent aircraft, and walked away.   Then he took a taxi to Orlando, to meet an anxious Richard Blankenship.   The two Colombians were dispatched to their hotel in a separate cab.

The memory of Bob Morgan's DC 3 surrounded by police cars haunted Andrew Barnes.   The last thing he wanted to do was to go back down to Winter Haven and face possible arrest.   He was certain in his own mind that by this time the Queen Air would have been traced, and the police would be waiting for them.   But Blankenship, made of sterner stuff, insisted. They ought, he said, to get that cocaine unloaded as quickly as they could.

"We go ahead and do that," Barnes recalled. "We drive down in a Volkswagen bus that's been left at his disposal down there, go to Winterhaven and approach the aircraft.

When we get there, there are two marked Sheriff's cars parked right next to the Queen Air."

The pilot's worst fears had clearly been justified. Suddenly, the older man saw it his way. "Hell, let's get away from here," said Blankenship. "Let's leave this aeroplane alone. They must have got the goods on it."

The pair went back to Orlando, where they were due to rendezvous with Carlos Lehder that night. There Barnes told his tale of woe to the Colombian, who was mightily unimpressed. He accused them both of being "sissy". Fancy allowing themselves to be scared off from unloading 300 kilos of cocaine, just because the police happened to be parked nearby! Were they men, or mice?

He, Carlos Lehder, would go and unload it himself. Carlos was not short on cojones, though his sense of discretion left something to be desired. He challenged them to come with him.

Blankenship, stung, agreed. Barnes refused and caught a commercial flight back to Fort Lauderdale. If Carlos wanted to get himself locked up, that was his own affair.

But Lehder was not arrested. Had he been, the tortured story of Norman's Cay and the Medellin Cartel might have been somewhat different. As it was, fortune favoured the brave, and the cocaine was unloaded from the Queen Air and carried away without incident. The Sheriff's cars were no longer there. Apparently their presence had been totally coincidental. Andrew Barnes, somewhat shame-faced, took a taxi from Fort Lauderdale to Winter Haven and flew the empty Queen Air home. It was now just an innocent aeroplane, but he never used it to smuggle cocaine again, fearful that it was being watched. It had, in any case, paid for itself a hundred times over. Ironically, this particular aircraft was confiscated by Customs some two months later when they found two marijuana seeds in an ashtray, left there by Carlos Lehder. But no charges were preferred.

* * * *

Lehder's operation at Norman's Cay was beginning to build momentum. Carlton-Reed and O'Hara were now installed in a villa beside the airstrip, complete with the comforts of home. Carlton-Reed, aged 47, was fornicating happily with a 17 years old girl friend named Michelle. O'Hara, 35, was having his solitude consoled by Cheryl, aged 16. In Barnes' words, the two girls were "a couple of weirdoes from California."

Both, however, subsequently married their boy friends, though the O'Haras, who had two children, have since been divorced.

Carlton-Reed, for good and personal reasons, did not fancy the idea of trying to infiltrate the United States. He feared his name was on the "wanted" list. But he was perfectly happy to make the hazardous trip down to

Colombia, leaving the second part of the operation to Andrew Barnes.

That was fine by Andrew, still sweating over his narrow escape in the Colombian farmyard, but maintaining a healthy contempt for the ability of U.S. law enforcement agencies. As far as he was concerned, making the brief trip from Norman's Cay to Florida was money for old rope. The carefree O'Hara, with no criminal record, was willing to act as co-pilot on both legs.

One small cloud had now formed over the organization. At the time it seemed fairly unimportant, but the consequences were to be far-reaching.

It happened like this: Carlos Lehder had arranged to meet Richard Blankenship, for some unknown reason, at a bar on State Route 84 outside Fort Lauderdale. He arrived to find Blankenship drunk. Very drunk, and totally out of control. The elderly man was swearing and cursing at everyone in sight.

Lehder was alarmed. If Blankenship was prone to behave like this whenever he had a few drinks, he was hardly the sort of man to trust with the dangerous secrets of the Medellin Cartel. He immediately instructed Andrew Barnes to remove Blankenship from any active role in the operation.

The Englishman did as he was told, relegating Blankenship to a few odd jobs, but not telling him the reason for his demotion. "I didn't want to offend him," he explained to me, "because I knew that offending him might have horrendous results."

In retrospect, it seems unlikely that Blankenship was fooled. The seeds of betrayal took a long time to germinate, but they were planted that day.

The next trip appeared to go smoothly. Lehder himself joined Carlton-Reed and O'Hara on the trip down to Colombia, stopping en route in Aruba, where O'Hara won $2,000 playing blackjack at the local casino. He supervised the loading of 350 kg of cocaine, and the party returned to Norman's Cay. There the shipment was transferred to a new twin-engined Cessna 206, and flown by Andrew Barnes into his old training base of Opa-locka.

Barnes merely joined the stream of budding pilots in the circuit, made a few touch-and-go landings to confuse the control tower, parked the aircraft and walked away to call a cab. He told them to send him a station wagon because he had so much luggage, and the taxi firm obliged. They drove Barnes and his twelve ether-reeking suitcases to his new house in Coral Springs, where he and Barbara stored the cocaine in the family garage.

"If you were just hauling suitcases it was a clean operation," he said. "The only thing that could have given it away would be someone smelling the drugs, or wondering why a pilot was travelling with twelve suitcases. There was a way around that: we just unloaded three at a time."

Andrew Barnes was feeling pleased with himself, but there was one snag. He had been supposed to fly into an airstrip at Ramuda Ranch, on the Tamiami Trail in the heart of the Florida Everglades, where Larry Greenberger was waiting for him; not into Opa-locka. The reason for the switch had seemed reasonable enough: Carlos Lehder had been late in arriving at Norman's Cay, necessitating a night flight for the second leg into the U.S.

Since the Ramuda Ranch strip was not equipped with landing lights, it seemed logical to Andrew to make the switch. Lehder had no objection, but no one troubled to tell Greenberger. The drug dealer sat in the middle of the Everglades all night, awaiting a plane that never came, and getting bitten to death by mosquitoes. He was not pleased.

A man of uncertain temper, with a bad cocaine habit, Greenberger was a native of Okeechobee, Florida, who had begun his criminal career selling drugs to the students at his alma mater, Florida State University. He was destined to become the Medellin Cartel's chief distribution agent in the United States, with intimate knowledge of virtually every drug wholesaler in the country. That was undoubtedly why, on September 19, 1988, Greenberger was found shot to death, execution-style, at his Okeechobee home. He was killed by a single shot in the back of the head, just days before he was due to be arrested on charges of Continuing Criminal Enterprise, which could have meant a life sentence.

Under such a threat, the likelihood of Greenberger talking to prosecutors and exposing the network was high. He had to be silenced. And he was.

Greenberger and Barnes had been friendly, with the Englishman taking his son to visit former's family at their western clothing store in Okeechobee, but he was not in a friendly mood when he arrived at Barnes' home next morning.

Greenberger was mad as a snake with hiccups after his long night vigil. He collected the cocaine and departed, fulminating. Then he put in a strident complaint to Carlos Lehder to express his total dissatisfaction with the way Andrew Barnes was behaving. This was not the first time that the pilot had failed to show up at the planned airstrip, and as far as Greenberger was concerned it ought to be the last. He wanted Barnes out.

* * * *

In the space of less than three months, Andrew Barnes had smuggled one ton of cocaine into the United States without losing a gram. This represented a wholesale value, in 1978, of $52,500,000 - and probably sold for ten times that amount on the street. For his services he was paid in excess of $200,000. He was, or should have been, a trusted servant of the Cartel. With things going so smoothly, it would have been logical for the arrangement to continue indefinitely, or until Barnes was caught, or crashed.

In the event, it did not happen that way. It was not just Greenberger's complaint after the third smuggling trip; Russ O'Hara and Jack Carlton-Reed, too, were whispering in Carlos Lehder's ear. They felt that he was showing favouritism to the Englishman, giving him trips that they would like to do themselves.

For whatever reason, Lehder summoned Barnes to Norman's Cay and told him to take a break from the smuggling business. He had plans to bring in other pilots, he said, who would be rotated in turn. Andrew might be brought back into the operation in a year or so. In other words, the young pilot was being let go. Fired.

There was another factor in the equation: Carlos Lehder, on taking up residence at Norman's Cay, had discovered that he not the first to have the idea of using it as a base. There was already a band of marijuana smugglers installed there; three pilots from Jacksonville, Florida, who were running their own small-scale operation out of the airstrip.

Rather than throw them off the island, for he was a man who believed in co-operation rather than competition, Carlos Lehder recruited them into his own grand scheme. It must have made more sense for him to have all his pilots based on Norman's Cay, rather than continue to use Andrew Barnes, who lived in Florida and might therefore be more vulnerable.

In retrospect, Lehder must have regretted this decision. The three men involved were Edward Hayes Ward, Gregory von Eberstein and Paul Sullivan Alexander. All were to be arrested in 1980, and all turned state's evidence against the Colombian. It was this that led to Lehder's indictment by a grand jury, his flight to Colombia and subsequent arrest, extradition and trial. No doubt it seemed a good idea at the time.

Ward, von Eberstein and Alexander were sentenced to long terms of imprisonment, but were subsequently released and are now hiding out under assumed names as participants in the Federal Witness Protection Program.

Andrew Barnes accepted the new situation philosophically, as well he might. By his modest standards, he was now, in his own words, "nigger-rich", and could do whatever he wanted. His debts on the C.46 were paid off - though he was to discover that it was never really possible to get out of debt with Charlie Bush, who was a genius at creative accounting - and he and Barbara had exchanged their apartment for the $225,000 house at Coral Springs.

He had no criminal record, and was not even under suspicion at this point. He even had his Green Card. It could have been a watershed moment for the 22 year-old Briton. His airfreight concern, now properly (or improperly) capitalised, was in a position to take off and thrive if he made the effort. Or he could have fulfilled his childhood ambition of becoming an airline pilot.

But Andrew Barnes, being Andrew Barnes, did neither. In his own words: "I didn't do a whole lot for the next two years. I kept working for Charlie Bush and kind of pissed my money away - which was to happen again later. I wasn't too productive. We went over to Europe once. I kind of got derailed.

"I should have done a lot of things, but I never did. We still had Caribe Air, and the C46 was down in Carrollton, Georgia. It had two zero-time engines on it, but I had in mind that I was holding that aircraft for a later date and I didn't want to have it all torn up hauling cargo. We put a long-range fuel system in it and a new fibreglass floor. We brought it up to really high specs, with expensive navigation equipment, practically like a modern jet. We had at least $225,000 invested in that aeroplane by the time we took it down to Norman's Cay."

The hiatus actually lasted for eighteen months. Until, in fact, Lehder lost his replacement pilots to the forces of law and order, and turned to Barnes once again.

CHAPTER SEVEN
The Littlest Smuggler

The call came in October, 1980. "One day," said Barnes, "I'm around Charlie Bush's office, and Charlie said a pilot had just swung by and handed him an envelope addressed to me. I walked in, picked it up and opened it, and there was a hand-signed note from Carlos. He told me to come over and see him, which I did a day or so later. I had to go to my brother-in-law's wedding in Philadelphia first, then I borrowed one of Charlie Bush's twin Beeches and my wife and I flew over to Norman's Cay."

It was a very different island from the one he had last seen: "When I got back there this time the whole place had changed. Carlos had built hangars over there on the runway - beautiful steel hangars. And there were a lot of people walking around with guns and walkie-talkies. There were several Colombians, all speaking Spanish, and two big impressive-looking German guys talking fluent German.

"When I landed there was a flurry of activity. As I remembered Norman's Cay, you could have crashed and burned on that runway and it would be two days before anyone came out to see what had happened. But now there were twenty people surrounding you as soon as you landed. It was a beehive of activity.

"This guy comes forward and says he's Rocky, the foreman there, and what is our business? 'What are you doing here?' he says. 'This is a private airstrip.'

"I explained that I was Andy; I had this letter from Joe. In addition, who are all you guys? They told me to wait in the office - they had built an airport terminal there with an expensively furnished office. This is all new. There are pictures of all the aeroplanes."

Carlos, too, had changed. The handsome young Colombian who had impressed Barnes with his authority and charisma was now high on cocaine and unstable as an elephant in must. None the less, he greeted the couple warmly, hugging Andrew and asking him to come back and work for him.

"We've made millions," boasted Lehder. "Since I saw you last I've made $100,000,000. I want you to drop anything you're doing." He handed Barnes $10,000 in cash from a shoulder bag. "Just get rid of all your commitments and come back in two weeks time and be ready to start flying. I have a brand new aeroplane in the hangar for you."

And he had. The couple walked over to the hangar, where Lehder proudly displayed a shiny blue and white Cessna 310, lavishly equipped. "That's your aeroplane," he said expansively. "It's a lucky one. Five trips already, and no problems. When you come back, you just take the plane and keep it."

In the meantime, he insisted on being taken for an aerial tour of his island, expounding the while on what he intended to do with it now that he was a wealthy man.

Carlos Lehder's plans for Norman's Cay would have sounded ridiculous in the circumstances, had they been uttered by anyone else. For this monomaniac, anything seemed possible. His grand scheme was to turn the island into a haven for the rich and famous; an exclusive hideaway where the international jet set could cavort in private. The incongruity of matching this enterprise with an ongoing drug smuggling operation did not seem to occur to him. He waved away the question when Barnes put it to him.

At some point, he said, he would abandon drugs and simply go into the hotel business. He would become legitimate. As a scenario, it was about as likely as Madonna entering a nunnery.

Carlos Lehder had come a long way from the 15-year-old immigrant to the United States who had begun his criminal career by exporting stolen cars from New York, and who had attended "university" in the federal penitentiary at Danbury, Connecticut. Now enraptured by his own product, he had acquired a terminal case of folie de grandeur.

Barnes began to notice other peculiarities about his boss. Looking around his luxurious house, it became apparent that Lehder had two idols in his life, both of whom he hero-worshipped. They were an unlikely duo:

Adolf Hitler and the late John Lennon, who would have been fairly appalled to find himself in such company. Memorabilia of both crowded the walls, and busts of the two were prominently displayed. It was odder and odder, but what the hell - Andrew Barnes was in it for the money.

"He was infatuated with John Lennon," Barnes recalled. "I was on the island the day that John Lennon got shot in New York. I didn't pay much attention to it. I used to hear him play John Lennon records and tapes, but I didn't have any idea that he was infatuated with this man. He literally wept when he heard the news that John Lennon was dead. Apparently he manifested this thing down in Colombia much more. He went around building statues of John Lennon. He had a bust built in the centre of Armenia, Colombia - got a world-renowned sculptor to build it and paid him half a million dollars.

"All the houses he lived in in Colombia, and in Norman's Cay, he would always have a bust of John Lennon and a bust of Adolf Hitler, together.

"I walked into his house one time, after Carlos left the island, and the busts of both had bullet holes through them. As did the ones in Colombia. I don't know whether he did it or someone else did it. The guy had become a little bit potty."

Barnes soon discovered that, irrational or not, Carlos Lehder had set up an extremely sophisticated operation on

Norman's Cay. The careless days were over. Now the registration numbers on the Cessna 310 were changed every week to confuse the authorities. Just about the only ones it never bore were its legal insignia of N2633U. Lehder would comb the Trade-a-Plane magazine, looking for a similar model aircraft that was on sale in Wyoming, California, or some other remote state, and pick out their registrations to use for himself. The phoney numbers were plastic stickons, bought from the Florida hardware chain of Lindsey Lumber.

The island even had a radio station, with its own call sign: Norman's Cay was "Dolphin Station", Lehder himself was "Dolphin". He loved that sort of thing.

The Cessna 310 was a six-seater aircraft and carried fuel for 12 hours flying. With a full load of fuel and the pilot on board, it could carry a thousand pounds of cocaine. It was later to be equipped with an STOL (Short take-off and Landing) kit at a cost of $22,000, making it an even more ideal tool for the job.

The extreme range capability of the Cessna was a feature that was to infuriate the Drug Enforcement Agency. Though the DEA was now flying its own airborne patrols in an effort to interdict the smugglers, the Citation jets and other aircraft they were using lacked the endurance to outlast the Cessna, especially at low altitudes.

"In all the time I worked for Carlos, I only got followed in one time," said Barnes. "Our deal with having such long range aircraft was that we could go all the way to Mobile, Alabama, attempt a landing, and find out that we had law enforcement present - either a Citation behind us or police at the strip. My guy on the ground had a radio. If he didn't like the way things looked - a funny car or something - he'd tell me and I'd go to an alternate airport. I always had fuel to return to Norman's Cay.

"If it was a DEA aircraft I would run down low on the deck. That drives the Citation nuts, because he has to burn so much kerosene to stay down there with you. I'd also slow the aeroplane up; dirty it up. I wouldn't necessarily drop my gear, but I'd drop my flaps to go into a slow flight routine. I could just sit there at 80 knots while he's trying to slow down.

"That happened to me once. I had to return to Norman's Cay. The Citation had to break off the chase. He just disappeared. They can only loiter for three hours at low altitude. I just waited until it was just dark, landed, put the aircraft in the hangars and changed the numbers again."

Carlos Lehder had it all worked out. He was ferociously successful at what he did.

The cocaine was now flowing in vast quantities. A Colombian crew was flying it into Norman's Cay from the Medellin Cartel's airfield in their home country, bringing 500 kg at a time in a Turbo-Commander designated Hotel Kilo. The drug would be amassed on the island, stashed in the hangars or hidden in caves, until Lehder had accumulated about 1,500 kg. Then the runs into the U.S. with the Cessna 310 would begin.

The flights were carefully timed. There was no more blasting out across the waves in the hope of avoiding detection. Instead, the smuggling runs took off at a moment when it was known, almost for certain, that there would be no aerial surveillance that day.

However, how could they know? The answer was simple enough: someone was paying a well-placed U.S. official to provide that information. Andrew Barnes was later to say in evidence at Lehder's trial that that someone was Charlie Bush, and the sum was $50,000. $50,000, he remarked, could buy a lot of information in Florida. It was all part of a smuggler's overhead.

Security on the island was tight. For all his wealth, Carlos Lehder lived in constant fear of being kidnapped by agents of the Drug Enforcement Agency or the FBI. Hence the presence of the two German bodyguards, Heinz and Jurgen - ex-paratroopers who had been trained at a special school for bodyguards.

"He virtually had these guys sleeping in his bed," Barnes said. "They were heavily armed with machine guns, and they kept a big Scarab speedboat there, fuelled-up and ready to go at any time to get Carlos off the island in a hurry. He became overly conscious about safety. He ordered me to fly in Dobermans, puppies, dogs from pounds. Just get as many Dobermans as I could grab my hands on. And that's what I did. I went and bought him Doberman puppies.

"For years after that, the whole airport was surrounded by Dobermans on long leashes, covering every square inch of that runway and apron. At the end there were probably about fifty of them. He was afraid a raid would come at night. So at nighttime they would put them on these runners so the dogs could run up and down the runway. They had various systems. They figured they had every aspect of that runway covered."

For the Barnes, the Norman's Cay operation rapidly became a family affair. All the needs of the smuggling band had to be transported to the island by air, including the jet fuel for Hotel Kilo. When he was not flying loads of cocaine in under the radar net, Andrew was using the Cessna and other aircraft to carry a rich variety of supplies. Apart from the Dobermans - an idea copied from his neighbour, Robert Vesco - these included quantities of penicillin to treat a raging outbreak of gonorrhoea brought to the island by a visiting party of Colombian whores. It was a varied life, and it earned Barnes a salary of $10,000 a month on top of his smuggling payments.

For her part, Barbara was made responsible for the smugglers' grocery shopping. The island's food bill was about $2,000 a week. Armed with bundles of banknotes supplied by Lehder, she made regular forays to the local supermarket to stock the drug czar's larder three or four times a week.

Carlos Lehder liked to live well, and saw to it that his men did, too. His English chef, Keith Goldsworthy, from Budleigh Salterton in Devon, was often required to prepare a lavish dinner for the entire population of the island, most of whom failed appear at table. "Goldsworthy told me: 'I hate doing this'" said Barnes. "Carlos made him prepare dinner for thirty people every day, and maybe only three people would show up. You are talking about excess to the point of ridiculousness. You are talking about cooking thirty rib-eye steaks and chicken, and preparing all these meals that would never get eaten. It was his job, he was getting paid to do it, but it was driving him crazy."

Goldsworthy had reached Norman's Cay by an odd route. Trained as a master chef, he, like many others of his generation, had been unable to find work in his own country. And so he obeyed the injunction of Britain's Conservative government and "got on his bike" to find it somewhere else. For Goldsworthy, this was easier than for most. While a student he had met and married a well-connected Colombian girl, in England on a student exchange program. She took him home, and he was hired straight off the boat.

The man who hired him was Jorge Ochoa, one of Lehder's partners in the Medellin Cartel. But, as it turned out, Goldsworthy's cooking was a touch too sophisticated for Ochoa's taste. In fact he couldn't stand it. And so, in a gesture of true friendship, he sent his unwanted chef to look after Carlos on his Bahamian island.

By all accounts, Lehder was not too mad about Goldsworthy's cooking either. But once they had discovered a joint taste for marijuana, and the Englishman had swallowed his pride and agreed to cook fish the Colombian way (ungutted, with the heads left on), the two got on well enough.

Goldsworthy found the experience frustrating, but rewarding. He was subsequently to be arrested in a Fort Lauderdale condominium, while "minding" 600 kg of cocaine, and was sentenced to 22 years in a federal prison. In retrospect, he may wish he had stuck to his pots and pans.

Even Andy Jr., then aged three and a half, was not left out of the enterprise. He not only accompanied his father and mother when they carried the steaks and wine across to the Bahamas; he also provided protective colouring when the incoming cargo was far less innocent. To this day, Andrew Barnes sees nothing wrong in involving his infant son in cocaine smuggling, even boasting that Andy Jr. probably holds a record as the world's youngest drug smuggler.

"He liked to fly," he explained as I listened incredulously. Was this Andrew Barnes, doting father?

"And it looked better when we came into the U.S. if it seemed like a family reunion when we got off the aeroplane. I wasn't doing any kamikaze air work. Getting in from Norman's Cay I was just flying the radar soft spots and doing touch-and-goes. "It wasn't a danger for him to be on the aeroplane. At least in my opinion it wasn't. That 310 was a brand new aeroplane. It was in totally tip-top shape, and we were flying daytime VFR."

The boy's mother was less sanguine. "I couldn't believe it," she interjected. "I gave him hell for taking little Andy. I remember I was very upset about that. Very."

True or not, her indignation seems to have made little difference, and there is some reason to doubt Barbara Barnes' veracity on this point. During the trial of Carlos Lehder in Jacksonville, Florida, her husband was cross-examined under oath by Jose Quinon, one of Lehder's counsel. The exchange went like this:

Mr Quinon: *On how many of those trips did you use your son as cover?*

Andrew Barnes: *The last three trips.*

Mr Quinon: *I believe you testified that you would get in some time in the afternoon, and it would take you three or four hours because you would do touch-and-oesat various airport?*

Andrew Barnes: *Yes, that was part of my procedure of flying.*

Mr Quinon: *And you also testified to flying with a rather heavy aeroplane, correct?*

Andrew Barnes: *Yes.*

Mr Quinon: *And in fact you encountered bad weather the second trip you took your son on, correct?*

Andrew Barnes: *That's correct.*

Mr Quinon: *And you also wanted to use Richard Blankenship as a sort of grandfather figure in case you got stopped by the police?*

Andrew Barnes: *That's correct.*

Mr Quinon: *Some of those trips, even though they took place in the afternoon, you ultimately delivered the cocaine sometimes at 2 or 3 in the morning. Correct?*

Andrew Barnes: *Yes. It's about a four-hour drive from Sarasota.*

Mr. Quinon: *And Blankenship and your son were with you all that time, correct?*

Andrew Barnes: *Yes.*

Mr Quinon: *Your wife knew you were taking your son on trips, did she not?*

Andrew Barnes: *Yes, he flew with me almost everywhere. Not just on these trips. He liked to go flying.*

Mr Quinon: *But she knew what those trips were, correct?*

Andrew Barnes: *That's correct.*

Mr Quinon: *In fact not only did she know you were using your boy at that time, three and a half years old, to do this; she came to pick you up one time and brought you another car in case you needed it, with the infant girl, Amanda. Is that correct?*

Andrew Barnes: *That's correct.*

Mr Quinon: *So your wife was not only willing to allow you to use little Andy on these flights, but also allowing the other infant and herself to come into the situation. Correct?*

Andrew Barnes: *Well, yes. The inference there is.... there's negligible danger in flying from Norman's Cay into the United States on these trips. It's not considered a dangerous or hazardous flight; it's routine. The danger comes in the flying to Colombia, so I didn't expose him to any risks that I thought were great.*

Mr. Quinon: *You didn't think your son, three and a half years old, was exposed to danger in the aeroplane under those conditions, with 300 kilos of cocaine?*

Andrew Barnes: *No, I didn't at all.*

Mr Quinon: *You didn't at all, because he provided you with a good cover so you wouldn't get arrested. Correct?*

Andrew Barnes: *Well, it wasn't the only reason, but it was the major reason.*

Mr Quinon: *And you were willing to do that: you were willing to use your little boy because you didn't want to go to prison. Correct?*

Andrew Barnes: *That's not correct. The aircraft I flew were not loaded to the point of danger. They were loaded within their operating envelope at that time. The aircraft performed flawlessly - it was a brand new aircraft - and I didn't see there was any prohibitive risk in taking him.*

Mr. Quinon: *Did you not think there was any danger involved in bringing cocaine into the U.S.? You could have been arrested with your young son present. Correct?*

Andrew Barnes: *That was one of the possibilities.*

Mr Quinon: *Possibility number two: You could have been ripped off. 300 kilos of cocaine amounted to how much money at the time?*

Andrew Barnes: *I have no idea. A lot of money. But I wasn't afraid of being ripped off, anyway. Nobody knew where I was going.*

Mr Quinon: *A few million dollars. Correct?*

Andrew Barnes: *Oh yes.*

Mr Quinon: *And all you wanted to do was use him for cove ?*

Andrew Barnes: *Yes.*

Mr Quinon: *And that's the reason why that little boy was with you, sometimes until 2 or 3 o'clock in the morning. A little boy of that age, while you were delivering cocaine.*

Andrew Barnes: *That's correct.*

Mr Quinon: *Then the truth of the matter is that you were willing to and did use your son to do that, just as you are willing to lie under oath to save yourself from all these years in prison. Correct?*

Andrew Barnes: *That's not correct.*

As that exchange makes clear, little Andy Jr. was an unwitting participant in three of the biggest shipments of cocaine moved by Carlos Lehder and his father. There were four suitcases in the nose, four in the aft baggage compartment, and eight in the cabin, weighing a total of about 450 kg. The Cessna 310 was so heavily loaded that it needed every inch of the Norman's Cay runway to get off the ground.

Those three trips alone, two landing at Sarasota and one at Clearwater executive airport, netted Carlos Lehder an estimated $67,500,000 on the wholesale cocaine market. In all, Barnes flew a total of five such trips over a period of two months in this second phase, without detection.

His reward was $600,000. "Carlos always paid us a cheap rate," he complains, "because Charlie Bush used to get a cut of everything. He was paying other crew members a lot more."

Still, at the age of 22, it was not bad for two months' work.

* * * *

Andy Jr. was not involved in the first two smuggling trips flown by his father after this return to Norman's Cay in December, 1980. These flights were remarkable for two things: their simplicity, and their audacity. Barnes simply loaded up the Cessna with cocaine and flew it into Fort Lauderdale International Airport. He parked it, fetched his Chevrolet Impala from the other side of the fence, and transferred the drugs into the car. All in broad daylight.

The cocaine was packed in duffel bags. There were too many to get in the trunk, so the remainder were carried openly on the front and back seats. No one at the airport seemed to notice anything unusual, nor did any patrolman remark on the fact that the Impala was so overloaded that it waddled down the road like a drunken duck. It was as through Andrew Barnes had a free pass to smuggle drugs. Carlos Lehder was pleased, but even he thought the Englishman was taking one chance too many. He chided Barnes after the first trip, and the pilot agreed to hire a hangar for the next one, where he could unload the cocaine in private.   He duly rented a building from Charlie Bush, only to find when he arrived that Charlie had parked another aircraft inside and it was impossible to get in.   Unperturbed, Barnes went back to plan number one, and got away with it once again.

This time he had borrowed a second car from Charlie Bush to solve the overloading problem, and together with a helper named Kiki drove the cocaine to a high-rise condominium in Brickell Avenue, Miami.   They left both vehicles in the underground garage and walked away.

A brief pause in the smuggling operation followed, while Barnes took the Cessna to St. Cloud, Minnesota, to have its STOL kit fitted.   The operation took about a month, but the Englishman was not left idle.   Carlos Lehder had a job for him which was very much to his liking.

At this point in time, Lehder had a problem; an embarrassment of riches.   Huge quantities of marijuana were accumulating back in Colombia, and the aircraft he was using were not big enough to move it to waiting buyers in the United States.   But Andrew Barnes, he remembered, had one that was tailor-made for the job - capable of hauling 15,000 lb. of cargo over long distances.

"We are ready for the C.46," said Carlos Lehder.

At last, Barnes had the opportunity he had been waiting for. All the investment he had poured into that old aeroplane was about to pay off, for as owner and pilot he could command a hefty fee. And to hell with Charlie Bush and his "cut." This time he was on his own.

Without further ado, he hurried to Georgia and retrieved the massive tail-dragger from the hangar where it had rested for almost two years.

Still in the red, white and blue livery of Caribe Air, the C.46 settled down on the Norman's Cay runway in a fully-stalled three point landing, the engines screaming in protest, as the entire population of the smugglers' island turned out to watch. Nothing that big had ever been there before.

No machinery likes to sit idle, and aeroplanes are no exception. There was quite a lot of work to be done on the C.46 before it could be pressed into drug-smuggling service. For two weeks, mechanics scurried to and fro from Florida, while Andrew Barnes fussed over the repairs like an anxious father outside the labour ward. He was worried, too, about the length of the runway. 3,000 feet was sufficient to land and take off when empty, but touching down with a full load on board, especially at night, would be a very different proposition.

Lehder saw the point. He also needed a longer strip for his Lear Jet, and arranged for the runway to be extended by two thousand feet at the northern end.

* * * *

While this was going on, Hotel Kilo was plodding to
and fro from Colombia, and the stash of cocaine on
Norman's Cay was mounting up. Andrew Barnes wiped
the grease of the C.46 from his fingers and went to
Minnesota to collect the Cessna 310. Barbara traveled
with him, and the pair returned to the island in the
modified aircraft, staying overnight with Carlos Lehder.
Parked outside were a station wagon and a Jeep, both
overflowing with cocaine.

They were ready to go again. In the intervening
month, Barnes had been doing some thinking. Perhaps,
after all, it was not so smart to unload cocaine in broad
daylight and carry it around Florida in duffel bags, in his
own car. He decided he needed a regular ground crew to
handle that side of the business, and he turned to Richard
Blankenship.

"He worked pretty steady for us before," he explains,
"and he seemed like a stand-up guy. It's hard to recruit
someone to go and pick up several hundred kilograms of
cocaine without knowing them. I didn't have anyone else
to use."

But there was a snag about using Blankenship. As
Andrew Barnes remembered only too well, the ageing
smuggler had been blackballed by Carlos Lehder because
of his erratic behaviour when drunk. Barnes solved this
problem with elegant simplicity: he neglected to tell the

Colombian the identity of his new ground crew. And Lehder never asked.

This time Barnes was given carte blanche to land wherever he liked, as long as the load was delivered to the correct address at the end of the day. Lehder probably realised, after his last experience with the Englishman, that he would make his own choice of airfield no matter what he was told, and he had, in any case, proved totally honest in the past. If honest is the right word.

There was one other change: having decided that a car full of duffel bags looked somewhat suspicious, Barnes suggested that they use suitcases instead. He bought new cases for each load - large, heavy-duty Samsonite baggage, purchased from J.C. Penney's. The store clerk must have concluded that his best customer was either an inveterate traveller, or very unlucky at losing his baggage on airlines. Andrew bought twenty-seven suitcases from him over a period of less than two months.

Complete with empty cases and his infant son, Barnes flew the Cessna to Norman's Cay and loaded up with cocaine. "The first trip I planned on unloading in Kissimmee, Florida," he recalled. "I sent Blankenship there with the same Impala I had used before. I sent my wife up there with an auxiliary vehicle because I wasn't sure how much load we would carry.

"But that night on television I heard about a big bust at the same airport, so I diverted them to Clearwater

Executive Air Park, close to Tampa. I had flown into that airport many times as an instructor.

"I told Blankenship to check into the nearest Holiday Inn to the airport. That was to be our M.O. from then on. If we got lost or could not find each other, the idea was that one of us would check into the closest Holiday Inn. That way we would always be able to find each other."

The arrangement went smoothly. In the event the extra car was not needed, and Barbara, who had brought their infant daughter with her, was sent home. Young Andy Jr., however, accompanied Barnes and Blankenship on the four-hour drive across Florida to the address given by Lehder. This was in Hallandale, a town of 25,000 inhabitants, between Miami and Fort Lauderdale. The boy was taken along for protective coloration, in case they should be stopped by the police.

"We got to the stash house late at night or early in the morning," Barnes recalled. "It was a 3 or 4 bedroom house on the intra-coastal waterway. Nice house, nice neighbourhood. I had been given an automatic door opener. I was to open the garage and drive the car in. We got into the garage, unloaded the cocaine and gave it to some Colombians, and then left." It was as simple as that.

The arrangement had gone so smoothly that Barnes and Blankenship decided to do the same thing again a few days later.   Only now there was to be one addition to their disguise.   Taking advantage of the difference in their ages, they decided to make it appear as though they were grandfather, son and grandson, all set for a family camping and fishing expedition.   The car was equipped with fishing rods, reels and coolers, to divert the attention of any inquisitive police officer.   Plus, of course, the infant Andy Jr.   Just how they would have explained away the nine heavy suitcases, with their 300 kilograms of cocaine pressing the suspension to the ground, is uncertain.   Fortunately for them, the necessity never arose.

There was, however, another problem that day: the weather.   A line of thunderstorms stretched across their path from Norman's Cay to the west coast of Florida. Rain lashed the windshield, and turbulence threw the tiny aircraft about the sky under the lowering clouds.   It was not a day to be flying at all, let alone with a three-and-a-half year old boy in a 'plane loaded to its limits with illicit drugs.   But like the U.S. mail, come rain or snow, sleet or tempest, the cocaine had to get through.   Andrew Barnes carried on.

Sitting in his Pennsylvania kitchen, he remembered the flight clearly: "I was forced to file an instrument flight plan in order to go through the Tampa terminal control area.   I couldn't go around it because of bad weather. Going through it, I had to communicate with the air traffic controller.   If I didn't, there was a good chance I would be marked as a violator and followed on radar, which would jeopardise my chances of getting that load through. I didn't want that to occur, so I tried to be as legal as I could, air traffic-wise. I landed at Clearwater air park and did a touch and go there, and proceeded to Sarasota, Florida."

The contact with air traffic control had posed another problem. He had had to identify himself by means of his transponder - a device which registers an identification number and details of the aircraft's position on the radar screen. This was a breach of his security. He had declared Clearwater Air Park as his destination, and therefore had to go there. But he had no intention of staying. The moment his wheels touched down, Barnes opened up the throttles and took off again.

"That was part of my routine in order to be devious, I guess," he said. "If anybody had been following me on radar I would throw them off my tail. As soon as I touched down I turned my transponder off and switched numbers. As far as radar was concerned, it made me a different aircraft."

With the weather as it was, that still left him the problem of finding another place to land. Most airports in the area were closed down. Still, the Cessna had plenty of fuel, and luck was on his side. The airfield at Sarasota, on the southern side of Tampa Bay, told him by radio that it was opening briefly. Andrew Barnes slid on to the runway with a sigh of relief.

Blankenship was summoned from the Holiday Inn in Clearwater, where he had been anxiously waiting for news, and the three set off once again for the house in Hallandale. By this time Andy Jr. was one very weary young drug smuggler.

CHAPTER EIGHT
Death of an Old Friend

The good times were rolling, but they were not to roll much longer. In December 1980, Carlos Lehder was warned to get out of Norman's Cay while he still could. And it was all the fault of Andrew Barnes, and a bulldozer driver who failed to do his job.

Lehder had become impatient at the slow pace of work on the C.46. He wanted that bird to fly. Work on the runway extension which would permit it to land relatively safely with a full load was not yet completed, but it was in progress. A dump truck and bulldozer were laying the foundations, and a pile of sand six feet high stood at the runway threshold. The Colombian probably concluded that since the cargo plane had got in once on the short track while empty, it could do so again. As it turned out, he was wrong.

Things were becoming tense on Norman's Cay at this time. Barbara Barnes described the atmosphere when she first began to go there as being "like a day out at the seaside." It was not like that now. Lehder's drug habit was beginning to affect his personality, feeding his megalomania. He strutted round the island like a king, always followed closely by his two ex-German paratrooper bodyguards, Heinz and Jurgen, and often by assorted women.

All the non-smuggling residents had now been expelled, most of them after being made offers for their property they could not refuse, and the hotel and yacht club were closed. Visitors were discouraged or, in the case of one elderly couple whose yacht strayed too close, killed. The romance of smuggling was dead.

"The first time I met Joe he wasn't that way at all," said Andrew Barnes sadly. "He had a lot more money now, and a lot more power, and it had obviously gotten to him. He was making $5 million a week, and he wasn't just transporting other people's goods; a lot of the cargo was his own. He was a big shot now, and he knew it. He talked about Adolf Hitler a lot. He had a lot of swastikas round the island. He was talking more about his German ancestry, and he didn't have much time for anyone else's point of view. He had become obnoxious.

"But I still kept working for him. Once you have all that money and you've ruined your reputation, it's hard to get away from that.

"That day we were working on the plane and he said: 'Come on, I want to see this big bird fly today. I want to see it all move today. I got a call from Nassau that the plane has to fly today.' Nigel Bowe had called him and said: 'you should do something with that plane instead of just leaving it there.' And that's what we did.

"We didn't want to fly that day, because there was a real strong gusting cross wind out of the south west which came right across that little short runway. That C46 has got a direct cross-wind component of only about 15 knots. The wind was steady at around 15, but it was gusting way above that. It was going to cause problems.

"Before I took off, I said to Carlos: 'that pile of sand at the end of the runway - you're going to have the guy move it, right ?' It was fairly early in the morning, and the crew was just getting ready to work out there. He said 'yeah', and he dispatched the foreman to tell them to move it, because I told him that when we land we are going to use every inch of the strip. I just didn't want that pile of sand sitting there when I came back in."

The C.46, watched by the entire population of the island, took off on its maiden flight from Norman's Cay. For two hours, everything went according to plan. Barnes stooged around the Caribbean sky with another pilot, Steve Stephens, in the left hand seat, adjusting the voltage regulators and checking that all the minor faults had been repaired. Lehder wanted to fly to Colombia the following week to pick up the first huge load of marijuana, and he was more than usually anxious that nothing should go wrong. Two hours later, satisfied, he turned for home.

Stephens, a former Air America pilot who had flown on covert operations for the CIA in Laos and Cambodia, was an expert on short-field landings in the C.46. Compared with the task of dropping the big aircraft into tiny fields bordered with tall trees, getting on to the 2,900-foot strip at Norman's Cay was no problem. Still, it would be a different matter when the plane was heavily loaded, and he agreed to instruct Barnes on the delicate art of making a full-stall landing at 70 knots, with the engines at maximum power. "It's a real hairy technique," said Barnes. "Your deck angle is just incredibly high. You feel you are about three hundred feet in the air when the main wheels hit."

It was certainly hairy that day.

From pattern height of a thousand feet, Barnes could see from the stiff windsock that the breeze was still directly across the strip, and still strong. The southern end of the runway ended in a sea wall, and since he wanted to use every foot of the tarmac and not risk an undershoot into the ocean, he set up his traffic pattern for a landing from north to south.

The undercarriage came down and locked with a satisfying clunk, and the C.46 lowered its port wing as it began a ponderous turn from the base leg on to final approach. As they neared the ground, beginning to flare-out for a three-point touchdown, neither pilot could see the threshold of the runway. With the nose at that angle, their sole point of reference was the far end of the strip, a thousand yards ahead. But their judgment was impeccable: the main wheels touched at the very end of the tarmac.

It was a pity that someone had forgotten to move the pile of sand.

The big aircraft shuddered as though it had run into a truck. It bounced high in the air, making recovery and landing impossible. Barnes and Stephens reacted instinctively, not knowing what had happened, but moving in concert to apply full power and set the mixture and propeller pitch for go-around procedure.

They relaxed as the C.46 staggered, clutched at the air, and began to climb away. Stephens reached down to the centre console and pulled the lever to retract the undercarriage once more.

This was a mistake.

The two men on board had no means of knowing, but when the landing gear struck the pile of sand the port wheel had been badly damaged. The mechanism holding it in place had broken, allowing the big tire to rotate sideways in the slipstream.

Now, when it was brought up into the engine nacelle, it could no longer fit snugly into its housing. Instead, it broke two engine mountings and crushed all the hydraulic fittings within the wheel well.

The C.46 was suddenly in real trouble. All power to the hydraulic ailerons was gone, robbing the pilots of lateral control. The oil tank within the nacelle had also been punctured, causing the port engine to seize up almost immediately. And to make matters worse, the right hand wheel had fallen back down into position while the left one remained jammed in its housing. Luckily, there was no fire. Much of the wing structure in a C.46 is of magnesium alloy, virtually impossible to extinguish once ignited.   Under these circumstances, the wings tend to fall off rather quickly.   Barnes remembered the moment vividly: "We had to fly that thing on the trim tabs.   We had elevator control, but no ailerons.   The fire bell started going off.   Everything that you can imagine was happening.   We were in a slow left bank of about 15 degrees, going round the island.

"Steve said, 'we've had it, Andy.' I said, 'I know.   I'm just trying to figure out where to set this thing down.'

 "He said: 'you know we've got our gear down on this side, don't you?'

"I said: 'Oh, crap!'   That big old tire was six feet tall.   I said: 'we're going to flip this baby if we go in the drink.' We were thinking about putting it back on the runway, but there were so many people standing there, and the villas were so close to the runway, and there were parked aeroplanes there.

"If that gear had been up we would have bellied it on to the ground, but I said: 'This thing is going to wander off into the woods, and we're going to run into buildings and cars and trucks, and those idiots are all going to stand there watching us while we're coming at them.'   So we ruled that out.   Anyway, a one wheel landing in a C.46 is very dangerous, because the thing sits up so high that you are almost cartwheeling on your wingtip when you touch down.

"Then a lagoon came up in front of us. It didn't take but a second. We got the wings level, using the trim tab, and we just went in, expecting to flip. But we hit the water so hard that it snapped the landing gear off. It had bled down, but it hadn't locked down, and when we hit the water it gave it a bit of leverage to snap it. If it had been locked down we would have been in real trouble.

"One thing I have to say about the C.46 is that it ditches well. It has that huge lower belly. The thing takes to water beautifully. We didn't even get our feet wet."

Andrew Barnes had had yet another narrow escape. But he had lost his beloved C.46, on which he had spent an estimated $225,000. Not that this mattered; at this stage of the game he could have bought six of the things and still had plenty of spare change. Of far more importance was the effect that the crash would have on the island's illicit activities. The wreckage, perfectly intact, now sat in that shallow lagoon like a beacon. It might as well have been a neon sign proclaiming "Here Be Smugglers".

Carlos Lehder must have cursed himself for ordering the C.46 into the air that day. So must Nigel Bowe, who reportedly suggested it was time that he put the big aircraft to use. For Barnes' plane was registered in the U.S., and any mishap to it therefore fell under the aegis of the National Transportation Safety Board. Within hours of the crash, Norman's Cay received a visit from a party of NTSB investigators.

The NTSB is not in the business of drug interdiction, but during the several days that they worked on the wreck of the C.46 the accident inspectors could hardly fail to notice that something a little strange was going on on Norman's Cay. It did not take a Sherlock Holmes to deduce that the fifty Dobermans were not being kept as house pets, and the German thugs were not carrying submachine guns to keep down the rabbit population. They went back to the mainland, and they talked.

From then on, the U.S. Drug Enforcement Agency began to take a keen interest in the goings-on at Norman's Cay. This was highly inconvenient, not only for Carlos Lehder but for the Bahamian authorities, who knew perfectly well what he was doing. Up to this point the eyes of the local police had been blinded by a comparatively modest payment of $50,000 per week. Now the Bahamian government was under intense diplomatic pressure from Washington to clean house. It was, to say the least, an embarrassment.

The authorities in Nassau responded by launching three police raids on Norman's Cay in quick succession. However, no drugs were found, and no arrests were made. This was less than surprising, Carlos Lehder having been warned in advance by the chief of police on each occasion. The cocaine was safely stashed away in a network of underground caves, and Lehder himself disappeared over the horizon in a fast speedboat to join Robert Vesco on Highburn Cay until told by radio that the police had departed.

The protection he enjoyed did not cease; it merely became more expensive. The pay-off to Sir Lynden Pindling and other members of the Bahamian government now rose to $100,000 per week, and Nigel Bowe was a frequent visitor to Norman's Cay in his private Piper Navajo, carrying the money back to Nassau.

All the same, it was becoming clear to everyone that Lehder's own presence on the island was becoming an embarrassment to all concerned. Edward Hayes Ward and his friends had been arrested and were singing their heads off to the FBI, and a Florida grand jury was about to hand down an indictment of the Colombian. It seemed wise to put some distance between himself and U.S. wrath, and so he flew back home.

It made little difference to the smuggling operation on Norman's Cay. Business carried on as usual, under the benevolent gaze of a detachment of Bahamian policeman who were now permanently stationed there.

As for Andrew Barnes, who, as owner of the C.46, might have been expected to suffer some heat as a result of the incident, he had another stroke of luck. It transpired that the aircraft's registration, transferred to Charlie Bush when he loaned Andrew the money for the new engines, had never been reverted to Barnes. It was therefore Charlie who had to answer some awkward questions. But then, he was used to that.

Before Lehder left the island, Barnes was to make one last smuggling trip for the Medellin Cartel. Two days prior to Christmas, the usual coded message came from Norman's Cay, and Andrew set off once more with his young son and a load of suitcases. Blankenship was sent to Clearwater Air Park to await the shipment, but once again the pilot changed his mind and landed at Sarasota. The reason this time was not the weather, but a nagging feeling that he might have been betrayed by a wiretapped telephone call or some loose talk by Blankenship in his cups. He and Andy Jr. landed without incident, but when he tried to reach Blankenship at the pre-arranged hotel the older man was not there. He was registered, but there was no answer from his room. Barnes was in a spot. There was an aircraft sitting on the open tarmac with nearly a thousand pounds of cocaine in the back, and no way of moving it. He also had a small, weary and fractious child to take care of.

"I figured Blankenship was mad at me," he said. "Maybe he had taken off because this was two trips in a row that I had left him waiting out at the airport all day. So I assumed the worst: that he had gone to Fort Lauderdale and left me there."

Nothing daunted, Barnes went to the office of the Jartran rental agency on the airport and hired himself a truck. It was none of their business what he wanted it for.   He paid a cash deposit, conscious that credit card transactions could be traced, and took the van back to the aircraft to unload the cocaine.   It was still daylight, but no one tried to stop him.   Then he went to a nearby motel to give Andy Jr. a chance to rest, and made one last bid to contact Blankenship.

This time his confederate was there.   Blankenship hurried over with the Impala, and the two men transferred the cocaine once more before rousing the boy and setting off for Fort Lauderdale across Alligator Alley.   It soon became clear, however, that they would not get there before the small hours of the morning, and Carlos had been complaining about his late arrivals at the Hallandale house.   It might, he said, arouse suspicion among the neighbours.

Barnes decided not to risk annoying Lehder again.   He pulled into the Holiday Inn at Plantation, just short of Fort Lauderdale, determined to spend the remainder of the night there and to deliver the cocaine in the morning. Blankenship was instructed to take young Andy home in a cab. The boy had served his purpose.   The cocaine, half of it on the back seat in full view, was left in the motel parking lot.

It was 3 a.m.   Barnes set a wake-up call for nine o'clock, and went to bed. Six hours later, he rose, took a shower, and sauntered out to the parking lot to complete a routine delivery of the contraband.   He was in for a surprise.

"When I walked out into the parking lot," he recalled, "it seemed like the entire Broward County Sheriff's office was parked around that car.   There were fourteen or fifteen police cars there, and they weren't just having lunch, either.   They had all their bubble-gum machines and flashing lights.   "Looking at this scene, I just assumed the worst: that my car had been surveilled and spotted, or it had been busted. I got out of there.   I took off."

Barnes fled in panic to Atlanta, Georgia, stopping on the way to telephone Blankenship and his wife to tell them what had happened.   He asked Blankenship to borrow his girl friend's car and drive by the Plantation Holiday Inn, to see what he could see.

"He came back on the 'phone and tells me: 'There ain't no car there any more,'" said Barnes.   "This made me even more certain that an incident had occurred.   I was just waiting to hear it on the news."

Andrew Barnes was not the only one to be perturbed. On Norman's Cay, Carlos Lehder was more than a little upset.   The team at the Hallandale stash house had notified him that the drugs had not arrived.   That load of cocaine was worth about $15,000,000, and the thought of losing it through the stupidity of an Englishman who left it in an open parking lot did not fill Lehder with feelings of brotherly love.

Rocky, the island foreman, telephoned Barbara Barnes to see what was going on. "Come on over and find out for yourself," she replied. "Andy said the car got busted."

Rocky flew to Fort Lauderdale immediately. There was a distinct aroma of suspicion that the Cartel had been ripped off, and Barbara was left holding the baby - both literally and figuratively. But she gave him the spare keys to the Impala, told him exactly where it had been left, and suggested he went to look for himself. He did. Blankenship's observation, and the Sheriff's Department of Broward County notwithstanding, he found the car exactly where Andrew Barnes had parked it. Still in the parking lot of the Holiday Inn. Still loaded to the windows with cocaine. It was untouched, and apparently unwatched. With only slight trepidation, Rocky unlocked the Impala, got in, and drove to Hallandale to complete the delivery.

Barnes was rescued from Atlanta by his wife, and flew over to Norman's Cay a few days later to get paid for the trip. But for once, he did not find Carlos Lehder in a generous mood. "I could tell he was a little disappointed," he said, "because he only gave me half the money I was supposed to get."

There was worse in store: Carlos told him to "go and take a break." As Andrew Barnes knew very well, this was Lehderese for "You're fired."

CHAPTER NINE
Almost an Honest Living

Nonetheless, the parting was cordial enough. Barnes, after all, had helped the Colombian out of a potential disaster. With mounting pressure from the authorities, and frequent buzzing of the island by the D.E.A. Citation jets, there was a daily threat that the tons of cocaine secreted in underground caves would be discovered and confiscated before they could be shipped to the mainland. Barnes had run the gauntlet and got the cargo through, whatever his errors of judgment. He owed him something.

Lehder, Barnes claims, offered to discharge the debt by asked him to come to Colombia and bring his wife and two children. There he would be provided with his own ranch, several cars, and private tutors for this children. Barnes refused. Ostensibly he was concerned about his family's safety, his children's education, and the fact that he spoke no Spanish. In reality, he said, he was getting increasingly worried about Lehder's irrational behaviour and wanted to sever their connection:

"Carlos was going nuts. He was snorting too much cocaine. He was confined to the island. He couldn't go to Nassau because he was on the stop list. He was there solely by paying off the government in Nassau, and they were getting increasing heat from the U.S. to get him out of there.

"I'm not a drug user myself, but apparently cocaine makes you very paranoid. It's one of the side effects. He was increasingly paranoid and drawn into himself. It seemed like he had started something, got into this whirlpool, and he couldn't get out. He was always in fear that the FBI or the DEA would come and kidnap him. He virtually had these German bodyguards, Heinz and Jurgen, sleeping in his bed. The machine that he'd created was about to devour him."

In early 1981 Carlos Lehder was gone, at least temporarily, from Norman's Cay. Though relieved of his drug-smuggling duties, Barnes stayed on for a while and plied regularly between Florida and the island. There were still groceries to fetch, fuel to carry, and errands to run. There was the occasional victim of a gunshot wound to take to hospital, fresh supplies of penicillin for the victims of venereal disease, and visits to Florida dog pounds to acquire ever more Doberman pinschers.

By now he was under suspicion from the authorities, who were casting a very leery eye on people who traveled to Norman's Cay, and delays of two or three hours in clearing customs were becoming commonplace. But still he had not been charged with any offence.

The departure of Lehder from Norman's Cay made little or no difference to the smuggling operation. Still under his direction from afar, it thrived mightily. The new terminal building, formerly the Colombian's office, was now serving as a barracks for the detachment of Bahamian police stationed on the island. Dreamily, from their vantage point beside the runway, the policemen watched the cargoes of cocaine come and go. And did nothing. That was what they were paid for.

More and more, the place was becoming an armed camp. All the former residents had now been run off the island, their homes occupied and vandalised by the fifty or more gun-toting thugs, mostly Colombians, who manned the watchtowers and patrolled the beaches to keep away intruders.

Passing yachtsmen were intercepted by a helicopter with Heinz and Jurgen riding on the skids, cradling in their arms the silenced Mac-10 sub-machine guns thoughtfully provided by Bob Morgan. Most took the hint. One elderly American couple who did not were later found shot to death, their sailing yacht, the Kahlia, drifting helplessly a mile off shore.

"Heinz and Jurgen would do that just to get brownie points," said Barnes. "Lehder wouldn't do that. I've seen people who came to him and said 'Okay, Joe, I've ripped you off. What are you going to do about it?' He would say 'just go on home and don't do it again.'"

This view of Carlos Lehder as a gentle forgiving soul is not universally held, and jibes oddly with Barnes' description of his paranoia. Nevertheless, the Englishman seems to believe it, blaming the Germans for most of the violent activity that went on at Norman's Cay.

"Their idea of law enforcement," said Barnes, "was to patrol round the island in this Hughes 500 helicopter, armed with these fully automatic silenced guns. If they saw a boat go past more than twice, the helicopter would go and check it out. One time they got three DEA guys, or what they thought were DEA - this boat just had too many antennae on it.

"These Germans were paratroopers. They would hover over a boat and board it from a ladder. These guys didn't have an ounce of fat on them. They were 6 foot 4 inch blond-haired blue-eyed Germans, who spoke fluent English. You could throw them out of an aeroplane and they'd just land running on their feet. They didn't do any drugs -they just drank like fish, and it didn't have any effect on them. They could drink gallons of beer and bottles of wine, and then go out and take a 20 mile run around the island."

One of the Germans, Jurgen, was wanted in the United States on a bond-jumping charge. He had been arrested while carrying $400,000 of Carlos Lehder's cash - the money was to be used to purchase an airstrip - and had skipped bail after the Colombian had paid half a million dollars to gain his freedom.

In spite of this, Lehder ordered him back to Fort Lauderdale to perform another errand, and Barnes was instructed to fly him from Norman's Cay in the Cessna. "Just be careful," said Carlos.

It should have been a simple trip, but it turned into a very close shave indeed. On board the Cessna, in addition to Barnes and Jurgen, were Barbara, Andy Jr., and a Canadian associate of Lehder's. And just for once the twin-engined aircraft, since it was not carrying drugs, did not a full load of fuel to outdistance any pursuers.

"I had flown fuel over there that morning, so we had virtually emptied the aircraft out except for enough fuel to get back to Lauderdale," explained Barnes. "Around Bimini, since I knew this guy Jurgen was hot and could not clear customs, I was real careful in getting on to the right course to avoid the radar. When we crossed Bimini, which is more than half way there, I did a left turn to check my tail, and I can see a teeny dot down there on the ocean, which I know right away is a Citation jet following me."

"He said he just had the feeling there was something there," added Barbara.

Said Barnes: "We had a dilemma. Theoretically we didn't have enough fuel to return to Norman's Cay, but I just turned round automatically. I wasn't going on to the States. That would be terrible. I figured we could land in Andros or somewhere like that.

"This Citation is now right there. We were eyeball to eyeball. They couldn't go slowly enough to follow us, so they were up, down, way ahead and way behind.

Ultimately they came right beside us and actually wrapped around us and buzzed us. We came within four or five feet of each other."

"I looked right into the pilot's eyes," Barbara added, her eyes wide at the reminiscence.

"You could see the colour of his eyeballs," said Andrew. Barbara: "They didn't know we were almost out of fuel. I had everybody take off their shoes and put on life jackets. I had everybody ready to ditch in the water. The Canadian guy was throwing up the whole time."

"Yeah, he got a little bit worried," laughed Barnes. "He wasn't used to all that stuff. I told him we were being followed by the DEA, and he was a little bit crooked himself. When Barbara went back and prepared everybody for a ditching it was just too much for the poor guy."

But once again the DEA, and the ocean, were frustrated. The Cessna made it back to Norman's Cay on the last drops of fuel, the engines cutting out before they could even taxi from the runway. They were safely back in their lair.

The quality of the company he was keeping during this period did not seem to bother Andrew Barnes unduly. None the less, he was becoming increasingly disturbed at the deterioration in Carlos Lehder when the Colombian made occasional visits to the island during his exile.

"He was becoming a different man," said Barnes. "He was completely changed. He asked me to find a good mechanic to take care of the boats over there, and I found this young fellow from Palm Beach. He had a couple of other Scarabs - he had a lot of boats over there - but he was having problems in keeping them running.

"So this kid went over there and screwed around with his favourite boat for a whole weekend. He replaced the head gaskets, did a top valve job on it, spent all day, all night and the next day getting this boat running. And he told Carlos before he went out in the boat that the problem might be that he was using the wrong fuel. He was using Avgas, and it should have been regular unleaded gasoline. The 100 octane is just tearing up the rings and burning out the valves. Don't be surprised, he said, if it doesn't run quite right.

"Carlos said he understood. He had been doing a lot of coke the night before. That's about $120,000 worth of boat, and this guy had gone through both engines completely. They went out for ten minutes and Carlos came back. I was on the dock. He looked real mad. He ordered the boat mechanic to pull up to the dock, and slammed right into it. Carlos ordered the boat mechanic off the boat and told everybody to stand back. He firewalled both the engines, with the transmission in neutral. He said: 'If you can't fix this boat right, nobody is going to fix it right.' He got off the boat and just left it running at full throttle. He said: 'just leave it there until it burns up.' That's how sick the guy was: totally irrational behaviour. That's just an example of what the cocaine was doing to him."

By the beginning of 1982, Andrew Barnes had reached a decision: he would cut loose from Carlos Lehder altogether. "My feelings were that this guy had gone crazy; a little bit potty," he said. "He had made all this vast wealth and now he just couldn't get away from it. It was going to catch him up and kill him, one way or another. He was wanted in his own country. He's mixed up with M.19 guerrillas down there, and he's got the U.S. government so riled that it's dangerous to be around him. It had become a cult. I looked at smuggling as a means to an end - to make money. He looked at it as his duty."

Of course, from Barnes' point of view, there was one other thing wrong with Carlos Lehder apart from his paranoia: he had cut the Englishman off from the actual smuggling part of the operation, where the big money was made. It was clear that the episode in the car park, the crashing of the C.46, and the deception over the employment of Blankenship had not been, and would not be forgotten.

The final parting, by Barnes' account, was amicable. There were no hard feelings. None the less, he was required to give back the Cessna 310, and handed it over to another Lehder pilot, Louis Fiero. Barnes knew Fiero well; they had learned to fly together and had studied in the same class at Miami Dade community college. Fiero was not a drug-smuggling pilot at this stage - he worked for a charter company and frequently flew Lehder about in a Lear Jet.

This inexperience may have led to the loss of the Cessna to U.S. Customs on his very first trip from Norman's Cay to the mainland. Fiero failed to notice that he was being tailed by drug enforcement agents, and though there were no drugs on board he was quite unable to explain on landing why the Cessna carried phoney tail-numbers. The aircraft was impounded, and Andrew Barnes was given the job of getting it back.

Say this for Andrew Barnes: he is not lacking in nerve. Here was a man who had smuggled more than a ton of cocaine into the United States over the previous few months, now suing the U.S. Government for the return of the very aircraft he had used for the operation. Acting on lawyers' advice, he formed a company called "Coral Aviation" and had ownership of the Cessna transferred to it. The aircraft had formerly been registered in the name of "Chelique IV", a Bahamas holding company named after Lehder's yacht, which held the title to all his property on Norman's Cay. The president of the company was Nigel Bowe, who dutifully provided Andrew with a phony bill of sale. Then, the paperwork completed, Andrew Barnes went to court, bold as brass, and asked the judge for "his" aeroplane back. And got it.

"The government was mad as hell," he said. "They suspected what it was doing, because it was operating from Norman's Cay.   They knew it was owned by Chelique. But we still got it back."

For the offence of carrying false registration numbers, the court imposed a fine of $10,000.   It was cheap at the price.   The $200,000 aircraft was promptly returned to Norman's Cay and put back into smuggling service.   It was eventually to be confiscated once more in Nassau, this time with a load of machine guns and cocaine on board.   It sits there still, slowly rotting.

This service completed, Andrew Barnes was once again his own master.   But from this point on, his pursuit of iniquity took a downward turn.   It was 1982, and he was 24 years old.   In the past three years he had made upwards of a million dollars, and though about a quarter of that had been lost in the C.46 debacle it still left a sizeable sum to play with.   Or should have.   There was a secret bank account in the Cayman Islands.   None the less, Barnes seemed to have a Teflon wallet.   "Nothing ever really stuck," he said.   "It's ironic.   A lot of money was going round, and a lot of it was being lost.   When you're a smuggler it's mad money, and you kind of know that.   Easy come, easy go.   If you lose $50,000 you don't really think about it.   It's not like you spend half your life earning it.   I was always in need of money."

His financial problems might have been fewer, had he not had a passion for buying aeroplanes.   It was an expensive hobby. Andrew Barnes bought aircraft as other men buy disposable razors, and kept them just about as long. Before he left the Lehder organization his private pride and joy was a seaplane, a Cessna 206 equipped with floats, for which he had great plans. These, naturally, had nothing to do with making an honest living: he intended to use it to smuggle cocaine into the U.S. by landing on Florida's Lake Okeechobee.

However, this ambition came to nothing. It fell foul of Charlie Bush and his creative accounting methods. Though Barnes swears to this day that he had paid the aviation dealer every penny that he owed him for help with the C.46, Charlie said he wanted more. So he took the seaplane, worth about $125,000, sold it, and kept the money.

Most men might have taken physical exception to this blatant piece of piracy, let alone Andrew Barnes who was rapidly becoming a hardened criminal. Charlie Bush was old and lame, having suffered from polio as a young man. But Barnes just shrugged, took his losses, and walked away to buy a twin-engined Beechcraft instead. It was indeed easy come, easy go.

Only now, with his Medellin connection severed, the "coming" was not quite so easy. There was no longer a smooth running organization behind him, with boundless resources to pay bribes and buy protection and information. Instead, Barnes was forced to rely upon fringe operators in the drug business for his commissions; men with even fewer scruples than himself.

Bob Morgan was the first to hire his services. Morgan had a fleet of DC 3's at an airfield near Griffin, Georgia. He asked Barnes to fly one of them to Colombia via Haiti, and to bring a load of marijuana back to Anderson, South Carolina. The landing in Colombia, at an airstrip known to the smugglers as El Labrador, was to be in darkness. It was quite like old times.

Barnes agreed to make the trip, together with a master cabinet-maker from Louisville, Kentucky, named Keith Pierce. Pierce, until his own arrest and imprisonment for smuggling a load of marijuana into Georgia, was to become his regular co-pilot. Also on board, in addition to several extra fuel tanks in the cabin, were two Cuban "kickers" in case they were intercepted and had to dump the cargo. The thought of landing at night in Colombia did not enthral Andrew Barnes, troubled by memories of farmyards and overweight take-offs. But he was a big boy now, with a lot more experience under his belt, and this time he found the strip without difficulty. As they flew overhead he watched the improvised runway lights flicker to life and began a cautious approach. Just one thing troubled him: there should have been radio communication with the ground, and there was none. He shrugged off a feeling of unease, lowered the wheels, and switched on his landing lights as the DC 3 entered its short final approach.

Suddenly, blue flashes came out of the darkness, punctuated with red flame.

"They're starting to light the flares, Andy," said Pierce cheerfully. But the strip was already lit. At that moment the two pilots heard the solid thwack of bullets striking the fuselage.

"Keith, they're shooting at us," shouted Barnes. "Go around!" His main concern, as the undercarriage was hurriedly retracted and the DC 3 roared back into the sky on full throttle, was that the Colombian soldiers who had lured them into an ambush might have hit a tire. He had forgotten about the two Cubans in the rear. He had also forgotten about the extra fuel in the cabin, stored in 55 gallon drums, feeding a bladder tank. The aircraft was a flying bomb.

Flying straight and level once more, and heading out of Colombian airspace as fast as the Pratt and Whitney engines would carry them, the two pilots went back to inspect the damage. They found wind whistling through an array of bullet holes that had turned the fuselage into a colander, but the Cubans had miraculously escaped unscathed. This was just as well: they had been spending their time since the shooting in patching the punctured bladder tank, which was leaking gasoline all over the floor.

Back in the cockpit, there was more bad news. Both engines were running smoothly, but the gauges showed that the one on the port side was losing a lot of oil. It had taken three bullets, one of which had pierced the pressurised oil tank.

"Our dilemma," Barnes recalled, "is that it's the middle of the night. We had some unknown damage to an engine, and we don't know whether the landing gear is intact. We could have gone to Haiti, where we had people, but it was a four-hour trip back over the open ocean. And we would be getting there before the airport opened. I turned on the ice lights and saw the whole wing was slick with oil. We must have lost five gallons already, and we are only 20 minutes into this flight."

The moment called for a stiff British upper lip.

"I said: 'I don't think we are going to make it, old bean. I think we are going to have to go on to Aruba.' Aruba is only 150 miles off our starboard wing. We had good ADF (radio direction finding equipment) pointing to it already, in case we have to go there.

"We discuss it for a while. The aeroplane is clean, except for the long range tanks in it. I said: 'what do you want to do, Keith? We can take a shot at going into Port au Prince and having to ditch this thing in the open ocean.' But we were still too heavy with all that fuel on board for single engine operation, so Aruba looked like a good choice. We talked to them on the radio, and were met with kind of funny gestures from the tower. But we were finally cleared to land. We were just a long-lost DC 3 in the middle of the night with no flight plan, landing there with bullet holes in us. We had that left engine feathered, bullet holes all over the place, and 55 gallon drums of fuel feeding a bladder in the back."

Not surprisingly, the authorities in Aruba decided there was something decidedly fishy about this DC 3. It had dropped out of the sky like the survivor of a World War II dogfight. There was, of course, no proof of ownership on board. There was not even an airworthiness certificate. Somehow, the Arubans just knew that Andrew Barnes was up to no good.

They surrounded the aircraft with machine guns, and kept the crew on board for an hour before deciding what to do with them. Finally, everyone was marched off to jail and thrust into solitary confinement.

It was Andrew Barnes' first experience of prison. But not, of course, his last.

CHAPTER TEN
Stepping Stones in the Ocean

Back in Florida, Barbara Barnes was desperate with worry. Until now, her husband's drug-smuggling activities had seemed innocuous. He had left her and returned with the regularity of a commuter on the Long Island express. Now, she was sure, he was dead. She paced the floor and drank Bourbon by the bottle while Morgan and Jack Leibolt, equally certain that the DC 3 must have crashed in Colombia or the Caribbean, took another aircraft and set out on a private search. They could hardly ask the Coastguard for help. After combing the whole area for a week, they finally learned through the grapevine that Barnes and Pierce were incarcerated in Aruba. Jail and death were the two common hazards of the smuggling profession, and the first was vastly preferable to the second. It was an occasion for celebration.

Not that Andrew Barnes was doing much celebrating. Conditions in the Aruba jail were less than luxurious, and communication was proving a problem. The official language of the island is Dutch, but most of the inhabitants speak Popumente, which is a pidgin mixture of French and Spanish. Barnes spoke neither, and nor did Pierce. Ultimately they managed to hire a Chinese lawyer, Shin Fat, after which things began to happen. Shin Fat, as good fortune would have it, was the brother-in-law of the judge, Chung Yong.

He was able to persuade his relative that since no drugs had been found on the aircraft, the two men were merely guilty of violating the air codes of Aruba. Shin Fat asked the judge to believe their story: that they had been on their way to Mozambique, via Recife, Brazil, and Dakar. As for the 110 strong nylon bags found by the police on board the DC 3, these had no connection with marijuana. How could he think such a thing? They were intended for the cargo of coffee to be picked up in Recife. There is, as the world knows, an awful lot of coffee in Brazil.

Whether or not the judge believed this absurdity, it worked. Barnes and Pierce were fined $10,000 each, and allowed to go free after being in jail for two months. Bob Morgan paid their fines.

This gesture was not wholly altruistic. Morgan had a job for Andrew Barnes. He asked him to get back in the DC 3, now repaired, and fly it to Colombia that very night. But for once in his life Barnes said "no". For the moment, albeit a very short moment, he had had enough of smuggling.

It turned out to be a wise decision. The Aruban police, who were not as gullible as they appeared, had put a "bug" on the DC 3 and notified the U.S. Drug Enforcement Authority. When the pilot who did take on the assignment landed near Belle Glade, Florida, on the shores of Lake Okeechobee, he found himself surrounded by federal agents.

Bob Morgan was also arrested, and was later sentenced to 30 years imprisonment on a conspiracy charge. 25 years of that sentence, Barnes calculates, were a direct consequence of his friend calling the judge "a red-necked son of a bitch."

Morgan had been a popular figure among the drug smuggling fraternity. The abrupt termination of his criminal career grieved his friends, but it certainly did nothing to deter their own activities. There was still money to be made, and in one way Morgan's departure opened a fresh avenue of profit for Andrew Barnes.

Bob Morgan's fleet of DC 3's, ideal for carrying marijuana, was now lying idle in Georgia and elsewhere. Their owner would not be needing them for quite some time, and Andrew Barnes was quick to step in to make an offer. He got the pick of the bunch for $50,000, with the promise of a further $50,000 from future profits. It was a steal.

Barnes and Pierce had become friendly during their enforced stay in Aruba. Now they decided to go into partnership, using Pierce's contacts among the Colombian and Cuban community to fix the drug deals. Their first few trips, however, were for a dealer named Julio Martin, since dead of natural causes. Martin had been introduced to Barnes by Charlie Bush. Who else?

The modus operandi was changing now. Interdictions of marijuana shipments directly into the U.S. were increasing alarmingly, and too many pilots were suffering the fate of Bob Morgan. Because of its greater bulk, as compared to cocaine, marijuana posed a problem. It was necessary to use larger aircraft, and to land them somewhere where the unloading of several tons of cargo would be unobserved. It was not merely a matter of handling suitcases. Such sites still existed, often on the land of suitably bribed farmers, but the attrition rate was rising.

The new plan was to wrap the bales of marijuana securely in waterproof material, and to drop them around various small islands in the Bahamas. There a fleet of boats would be waiting, the rendezvous arranged by radio, to pick up the floating bales and bring them into Florida by sea. This was reckoned to be far less risky, especially for the pilots.

This was fine with Barnes and Pierce. They would be able to operate entirely outside the United States, basing the DC 3 at West End in the Bahamas and using Port au Prince, Haiti, as their actually jumping-off point. First, there was work to be done. Barnes collected Morgan's aircraft from Griffin, Georgia, and flew it to Port au Prince where the two men stripped out the interior furnishings. Two thousand pounds of weight saved in the cabin meant another ton of marijuana to be carried.

Their first trip was aborted when the weather off Barge Cay, south of Bimini, proved too rough for the fast speedboats to put to sea.   But a week later, after sitting out the gale in Port au Prince, they headed back down to Colombia once again.   Their destination was an airstrip known as Panorama, in the northern Magdalena province of Colombia, where they were scheduled to land at dusk. This would enable the drugs to be loaded during the hours of darkness, ready for a dawn take-off.

The strip was easy enough to find, but difficult to approach unseen.   There was a choice: fly high, so that police on the ground at Santa Marta would not spot the aircraft, or fly low to avoid detection by the radar at Barranquilla.   Barnes chose the former.   He was wrong. Glancing out of the cockpit window as he began his descent, he was horrified to see a Mirage jet fighter of the Colombian air force flying in formation on his wingtip.

"I didn't know what that crazy guy was going to do," he said.   "Whether he was going to shoot us out of the air, or what."

Either way, there was not much Barnes could do about it.   The jet disappeared from sight, and with the hairs prickling on the back of his neck he got the DC 3 on to the ground as fast as possible, expecting a burst of cannon fire to rip through it at any moment.   But nothing happened.   The cargo plane bounced to a halt on the rough dirt strip, and Barnes began shutting down the engines hastily while Pierce got the rear door open and the ladder down.   Neither had any wish to be caught in so clear a target on the ground.

Barnes looked up from his switches and knobs.   "I see everybody running.   Everybody is fleeing for the woods. I look up and I see this Mirage.   He's gone right around the back. I thought he was gone, but he was coming back.

"So I get out of my seat and run to the tail of the plane and just jump out.   All I can hear is the sound of bullets ripping through the ground, and this thing goes soaring right over my head.   It seemed about eight feet above my head.   I was so deaf from the shock and the percussion of that aeroplane I couldn't think.   I just fell down.   It seemed like I got up in a daze about a second or two later and started running for the woods too."

After a single pass, the jet zoomed skywards and apparently headed back to its base.   No one on the ground had been wounded or killed in the attack, and Barnes was astonished when he emerged from the woods and inspected his aircraft to find that the DC 3 was also without a single bullet hole.   He was puzzled.   It had been a perfect target; how could the guy have missed?

The explanation proved to be simple: "We found out later that night," Barnes said, "that it was just a warning. The guys we were dealing with had to pay $30,000, otherwise that pilot was going to come out in the morning and strafe our aeroplane.   It was the air force way of letting the guys on the ground know that they needed a pay-off. They weren't going to shoot us or the aeroplane,

174

but you'd have had a hard time convincing me of that at the time."

Grumbling but resigned, the Colombians paid their dues to the air force. Graft and corruption are part of the smuggling way of life. It was frustrating next morning to find that the airstrip, which lay in the valley of the Magdalena river, was covered in thick fog. Visibility was no more than a few feet. The Mirage could never have made an attack.

The Colombians insisted that they took off at once. Barnes demurred. The DC 3, as usual, was badly overloaded. It had 5,500 lb. of marijuana in the cabin, plus full wing tanks, 500 gallons of extra fuel, and a pair of Cuban "kickers" to unload the cargo if and when they reached their destination. To attempt a take-off in thick fog from a short and soggy airstrip was tantamount to suicide.

"Go", said the Colombians. They feared that an army ground patrol might be on the way, looking for its own piece of the action. Expenses were high enough already.

Barnes went. "Gear up, Keith," he shouted, as the DC 3 lumbered off the ground and poked its nose into the impenetrable murk. Nothing happened. Pierce had left the undercarriage locking pins in place.

Now, to add to their other troubles, they would have to fly all the way home with the wheels down. This not only added extra drag to an aircraft already beyond its maximum permitted weight, but it effectively ensured that if they had to ditch in the ocean the DC 3 would flip on to its back and kill them all. Barnes swore. The only way of removing those pins would be to return to the strip and land. But the runway had long since disappeared behind them, and there was no way of finding it again in the fog. They would have to go on and hope for the best.

Somehow the over-strained engines held together. At 3,000 feet they broke into clear air and headed north across the Caribbean. For choice they would have overflown Haiti on their way to the Bahamas, but with this load on board there was no question of gaining sufficient altitude. Unless they wanted to fly into a mountain, they would have to go around the Haitian coast. And that meant exposure to detection by the powerful U.S. radar station at Cuba's Guantanamo Bay if they passed to the east of Haiti, and by a new installation in the Dominican Republic if they flew eastward and took the long way round.

The net was tightening. With all legitimate flights required to file an instrument flight plan, it was not hard to identify illicit aircraft. In Barnes' words: "when they pick up a target that ain't talking to nobody, they send someone out to investigate."

And sure enough, when he climbed into the navigator's Plexiglas dome on the DC 3 - a relic of an earlier age, but useful for seeing what it going on behind you - there was a Drug Enforcement Agency Citation jet. Right on their tail.

At this point the smugglers' options were strictly limited. They were loaded down with enough marijuana to send fifteen regiments on a trip to the moon, and it was broad daylight. Whatever they did was going to be closely observed, and wherever they landed the police were going to be waiting. It was Hobson's choice.

Barnes and Pierce decided to go ahead and make their scheduled air drop at Orange Cay, south of Bimini, as though nothing was amiss. It was not just bravado. At least, they may have reasoned, if the waiting boats picked up the cargo and managed to get clear, they would get paid for the trip at the end of the day. Where they were likely to be going, a little money would come in handy.

By the time they reached the dropping zone they had not one tail, but two. The Citation had peeled off and left the chase to two other D.E.A. aircraft, a Navajo and an Aerostar. On the water, the Cubans manning the pick-up boats were delighted as they saw this aerial flotilla approach - they thought all three were carrying marijuana.

But it was only Andrew Barnes who made the bombing run; shedding bales of marijuana in a steady stream as the DC 3 roared over the boats at scarcely a hundred feet. The other two aircraft merely sat back and filmed the whole operation.

The sight was spectacular: almost a hundred bales, each weighing about 60 lb., turned slowly in the air as they were kicked from the cargo door. They hit the water in a shower of spray, bouncing like stones skimmed on a village pond before coming to rest and floating, fat and black on the blue sea. Through the viewfinders of their movie cameras the federal agents could hardly believe their eyes. This was going to be one beautiful bust.

Their task completed, Barnes and Pierce continued north to West End, roughly 75 miles distant, on the tip of Grand Bahama Island. The D.E.A. aircraft followed them every inch of the way. It was a busy journey for the smugglers, who spent the time cleaning out the DC 3 as though it was about to be entered for a concourse d'elegance. By the time they landed there was not a leaf, not a seed, not a trace of marijuana on board.

Barnes taxied up to the ramp, the Navajo and the Aerostar close behind. He wore his most innocent expression. There, waiting for him, were Julio Martin and some of his associates.

There were also a few Bahamian police and customs officers, but since these had all been paid off, and were in fact waiting to give him the necessary documents to legalise the flight, Barnes was unworried.

The police who came clambering out of the DEA Navajo as it slewed to a stop beside him were a different matter. They were carrying guns. Barnes and Pierce did as they were told. They put up their hands, lay on the ground, and emptied their pockets.

"What's going on?" asked Barnes, feigning ignorance. "We just came from Bimini."

For some unaccountable reason, no one believed him. The pair were arrested, handcuffed, and taken to the local police station for interrogation. Barnes refused to admit a thing. In spite of the presence during the interview of DEA agent Charlie Overstreet, who had watched the whole thing and had undeveloped film to prove it, he denied categorically that he dropped any marijuana off Orange Cay. Why, he said, brandishing his false documents, he had papers to prove that he had merely flown from Bimini to West End.

"Bullshit!" shouted Overstreet, banging his fist on the desk. "They dropped so much shit in the water, you could walk on the bales from Bimini to Miami."

Barnes and Pierce were taken down town and thrown into jail, where they spent an anxious 72 hours. Then they were released. Everyone knew they had made that air drop, but under Bahamian law there can only be a conviction if traces of drugs are found on the aircraft. And thanks to hard work and forethought, the DC 3 was clean.

It was also impounded, but that was a minor problem. After $10,000 had been slipped to Nigel Bowe, the aircraft was miraculously returned to its owner.

The smuggling firm of Barnes and Pierce was back in business. Financially, however, they were not doing too well. The agreed fee for the flight to Orange Cay was

$200,000 for Barnes, as pilot and owner of the aircraft, and $50,000 for Pierce as co-pilot.   In the event they got nothing, because DEA helicopters prevented the speedboats from picking up the marijuana.   More than two tons of the drug went drifting away into the Caribbean, or so Julio Martin claimed.

CHAPTER ELEVEN
The Gentlemen Pass By

By 1983, drug smuggling was no longer a gentleman's occupation. Of course it never had been, except in the minds of those who saw it in terms of high adventure and derring-do, but now it had slipped several notches down the social scale. The pilots still congregated at various bars around the Caribbean, notably the Snake Pit in Port au Prince, Haiti, but the drinking was more desperate and the jollity more forced. Old faces were beginning to disappear. Most of them had been veteran fliers, ex-service pilots down on their luck, or men like Barnes who began by trying to make enough cash to rescue legitimate businesses. Now, increasingly, they were being lost to crashes or the forces of law and order. The Caribbean bars had begun to resemble air crew messes during the Battle of Britain; places where every party was a wake for absent friends.

A few, a very few, had had the good sense and good fortune to take their money and get out. They were a tiny minority. Most would promise themselves "just one more trip", until the moment when they found themselves in handcuffs or an engine failed on take-off from some remote airstrip.

The men who replaced them were mostly younger and often lacking in flying experience. Some did not even have private pilot's licenses, picking up their skills from flying in the right hand seat and then chancing their luck on their own. They, like the dealers who arranged the shipments, were drawn like sharks to the lure of easy money.

It was a feeding frenzy of greed, and there was certainly enough cash to attract the predators in the pellucid waters of the Caribbean and Bahamas. There was also blood. Stepped-up law enforcement, especially in the Bahamas, meant that virtually all flying now had to be done at night. The hazards were enormously increased. Night landings and take-offs in Colombia; long night flights over the empty ocean; night drops from low altitude to waiting boats off the islands; subsequent night landings at a remote home base. Each contributed to the growing toll of aircraft and pilots, especially those who lacked experience.

"It's a terrifying ride," said Barnes. You go down to Colombia, and you think about all the stuff that's going to happen on the way back. You get down there, and you're thoroughly relieved that you found the airport and you're on the ground and getting refuelled. Then the anticipation begins for that heavy take-off at night. And you get into the air, and the aeroplane makes it to altitude, and you take a breather.

"You're all right for a couple of hours, until all of a sudden you've got to start thinking about the landing. Are those twerps going to be there? Are there going to be police on the ground? Are there going to be choppers there? You're worried about going to jail, and you're more worried about actually getting the aeroplane on the ground in one piece. And then when all that's over you've got to move the plane again.

"Then your apprehension builds again, because you've got to clear customs somewhere to get this thing back legally somewhere. It's really a roller coaster ride of emotions."

Andrew Barnes was discovering something else: that he might have made a grave financial error in severing his connection with Carlos Lehder. For all Lehder's volatility and excess, he had one virtue that endeared him to those who worked for him. He always paid, and he paid in full. In that sense, to give the devil his due, he was a nicer class of criminal.

"He paid all the time, and you get spoiled by that," Barnes recalled wistfully. "After that I dealt mostly with Cubans, and the Cubans are a totally different kettle of fish from the Colombians. The Colombians pay. Their job is to see that their stuff gets there, and everybody walks away happy so that you'll work again.

"The Cuban figures he is going to rip everything off, because you ain't going to work for him no more anyway. His idea is to cut everything to the bone, and maybe rip the whole load off and run. That's the Cuban mentality. Colombians live down there; they grow the stuff. It's an industry to them. They want to see a pilot happy and keep coming back. Cubans are different, and I never could run into a good bunch of Colombians again after Joe Lehder. The Cubans had infiltrated so much of this business that the Colombians were virtually all down there, and the Cubans up here. At that point I had no means of getting back with Joe again."

Julio Martin, Barnes' new employer, was a crook of a different colour. The Cuban refugee was not a nice person at all. In all, Barnes made three trips for Martin in the DC 3 he purchased from the incarcerated Bob Morgan, switching to night drops off the north coast of Grand Bahama Island after the fiasco at Orange Cay.

The bales of marijuana, double-wrapped in hessian and then enclosed in a nylon bag and several heavy-duty garbage bags, now carried illuminated plastic tubes to enable them to be found by the waiting boats. From the air it looked like the fourth of July as they bounced end over end for thousands of feet.

The boats themselves were invisible, and in constant danger of being sunk by the falling bales, which even from a height of only 500 feet had the power and velocity of non- explosive bombs. Once Barnes did sink a boat, but this was not his main concern. His worry was that he was not getting paid. At least, not the $200,000 per flight that he considered his due. Instead, using one excuse or another, Martin would fob him off with $25,000 or $30,000.

"They would give you enough money so that you wouldn't shoot them, but after that they wouldn't pay you," he said.   "I wasn't the shooting type, and they knew that."

But even the non-belligerent Barnes had his patience tried by what happened next.   He had finally had his fill of Julio Martin.   Both he and Keith Pierce were determined not to fly for the Cuban any more; the rewards were not worth the aggravation or the risk.

But at least the small payments he received for the last two flights had been sufficient for him to complete his deal with Bob Morgan, and the DC 3 was now his.   He decided to leave it parked at West End airport, Grand Bahama, where the authorities were bought and paid for, and return to Florida until something turned up. Destitution was not exactly staring him in the face - there was no need to earn an honest living just yet.

But Barnes had underestimated Martin, who reasoned that a perfectly good drug-smuggling aeroplane should not be allowed to go to waste.   All he needed was a crew to fly it. The fact that the DC 3 did not belong to him and he had no permission to use it were matters of little or no consequence.   With Barnes' record, the Englishman was hardly likely to go to the police and complain.

Finding a crew was no problem for Martin.   Finding a *competent* crew was another matter.   The pair he chose, names unknown, had not bothered to brief themselves on the auxiliary fuel system that Barnes had installed in order to be able to reach Colombia.

There was a bladder tank to be filled, and they filled it. There was a cross-feed pipe to which it had to be connected, and they connected it. What they did not know, however, was that the latter operation had to be performed in a certain sequence, otherwise air would enter the fuel lines and engines would be unable to suck gas from the reserve tank.

This was unfortunate. On the flight down to Colombia the DC 3 ran out of fuel just short of the South American coast and ditched in the sea off Santa Marta. The fate of the crew, as with most smugglers who disappeared from the face of the earth during this period, is not recorded. But the seas in that area are not kindly.

Two days later a telex message was sent to Andrew Barnes, care of Charlie Bush. It was from the U.S. Consulate at Barranquilla, regretfully informing him that his plane had crashed and offering to provide further details on request. Barnes decided not to accept the invitation. There was nothing to be done, the DC 3 was lost, and the less contact he had with officialdom the better. Instead he set off for Miami, intent on tracking down Julio Martin and extracting payment for the value of the stolen aircraft. It was a forlorn hope. Martin had wisely disappeared.

Once again, Andrew Barnes was without an aeroplane. In the past year two had been stolen, and one he had crashed himself.   Their total value approached half a million dollars.   Perhaps, he thought, I ought to be in some other business.   It was a good thought, if a little late in crossing his mind, but it would not endure for long. The business he chose was trucking, and at first it made good money.   However, a succession of dishonest drivers who either stole his tires, or abandoned the truck at the end of the road, soon convinced Barnes that there were easier ways to make a living.   Not honest ways, but easier.   Once again he began looking around.

"I just got into a bad habit," he said disingenuously, "of looking for a smuggling trip every time I needed money.   It's so easy to make the money when they pay you.   You're taking a lot of risk, both physically and of getting thrown into jail, but I seemed to be able to rationalise that.   It's a kind of disease, I guess."

Which was how he met John Torres.

As a judge of character, Andrew Barnes was proving to be in a league of his own.   Apart from his recent experience with Martin, it was not as though he knew nothing of the likely consequences of associating with the likes of John Torres.

All Cuban drug dealers had a reputation among the smuggling fraternity for double-dealing, ripping off loads, and cheating pilots at every possible opportunity.   None the less, Barnes agreed to join with Torres in a partnership that lasted, on and off, for more than three years.

It was to be his great undoing.

*   *   *   *

At first, things went relatively smoothly. Torres claimed to own a DC 3 in Haiti and sent Barnes down to inspect it. The aircraft proved to be mechanically unsound, with serious electrical problems in one engine, but this was a minor inconvenience. They could always find aeroplanes; Charlie Bush would provide. And so, at the controls of a twin-engined Beechcraft, Andrew Barnes began once more flying marijuana out of Colombia and dropping it at various points close to the United States. Ponce, at the southern tip of Puerto Rico, became a favourite spot, but the Bahamas continued to get their fair share. After each trip he would return to a base on South Caicos Island where, according to Barnes, "We had the whole island paid for, from the police on down."

He had a new co-pilot now - a Californian named Curtis Emmer, whom he met in Haiti. The two men were similarly driven. In Emmer's case, it was the need to rescue a failing marina business in Fort Lauderdale that had got him into the smuggling racket, though by the time he met Barnes this ambition had long past. He was already a wanted man in the U.S., having jumped bail on a variety of charges, and for him there was no way back.

Colourful is probably the best word to describe Curtis Emmer. A qualified sea captain, he was once rammed by whales while sailing a catamaran across the Pacific. Subsequently, while flying a cargo of illegal aliens into the U.S. - an occupation he interspersed with carrying marijuana for associates of Carlos Lehder - he crashed in the Florida Keys when attempting to avoid a helicopter and took the control column through his stomach. It was one of several major accidents.

"Curtis is a survivor," said Barnes admiringly, "but he has problems with the aeroplane."

He was also a heavy drinker, as by this time was Barnes himself. There was no rule of "24 hours between bottle and throttle" for these two. They would drink merrily all the way down to Colombia, and most of the way back. With a few glasses on the ground to keep their spirits up.

"When I was smuggling stuff I was always drinking," admitted Barnes. "I was always high. I can stop drinking. I can go home and stop for a month, but it seemed like when I was working it was just going hand in hand with smuggling. Some people did drugs, I did booze. Drinking and flying always went hand in hand together.

"I used to use alcohol to keep awake on these long night ocean passages. Alcohol puts some people to sleep, but it keeps me wired. I just concentrate on the flying. I put out of my mind that the Colombians might be down there to shoot us, or the Citation might follow us back. It kept me awake. That's why I drank."

Barnes boasts that he never had an alcohol-related accident while flying. The age of miracles is clearly not past.

In Colombia, they were now using a strip known as "the Lighthouse" on the northern tip of the Guajira Peninsula. It was not a safe place. From the sea, the approach was marked with the bones of wrecked ships, mostly drug smugglers, who had failed to observe the warning of the light. The strip itself, pointing straight out to sea, was flanked with the marked graves of more than a hundred pilots and crew who had crashed on take-off or landing. A bulldozer was permanently on site to haul away and bury the wreckage.

The Lighthouse airstrip was owned by a man called Jacobito, and staffed by ten or a dozen heavily-armed Colombians, using local Indians to load the cargo. For many months, this was to be Andrew Barnes' main port of call, and the scene of many dramas.

"It's a hell of a place," Barnes recalled. But he waxed almost lyrical about it: "We'd spend the night there, loading the aircraft up, generally bullshitting. It's beautiful down there at night. Like being on a boat. You can hear the sea crashing off the shore. It really runs high. The sky is totally clear; there are no clouds down there; it's desert. Totally beautiful, but also kind of scary at the same time.

"The closer you get to take-off time, the more the tension builds in your stomach. When you first get down there you're relieved to get out of the plane and stretch your legs and have a drink and relax. Every time I went down with Curtis he'd be tearing a bale apart to get a joint out of it. You do whatever you can to relax, but as you approach take-off time you can cut the air with a knife. You know you are going to be blasting off into the dark blue yonder with no hope of return. And anywhere you go, you are going directly to jail. So the older the aeroplane and the heavier the load, the more the tension builds up to a kind of crescendo. To the point where, when you're ready for take-off, and a Colombian does something stupid like knock a smudge-pot over, you could just about kill somebody. You really want to get out of there."

For Barbara Barnes, at home with two young children, none of this was too much fun any more. She spent hours walking the floor, chain-smoking and downing bottles of bourbon, waiting for her husband. Wondering if she would ever see him again.

"It wasn't like that in the beginning," she said. "On the later trips, every time he left the house I had this horrible, horrible feeling of impending disaster, which I had never had before.

"It got to the point where I would try not to worry up to a certain time. And then, as that time approached and I knew I should have heard from him or somebody, I would start coming unglued. I hated it. I don't know how I stood it.

"It would take him a while to unwind. Then he'd tell me of this or that incident. But he always removed me from being directly involved. All I got was his feedback, and the way he would tell things was like he had a ball. All that danger was there, and I knew it, but he always tried to keep me shrouded in this sense of fun. I could see it was not really like that, but it was just the way he told it to me."

Barbara Barnes was not naive. She was a pilot herself. She knew. "He would come back and sit there with his gin and talk to me, and tell it like it was a wild adventurous tale. In fact, I knew he had almost been killed. Again."

Andrew Barnes recalled one of those tales for me. "Curtis and I went down there one time, and Curtis was rip-roaring drunk before we arrived," he said. "So he straightens out with smoking marijuana. But these guys had been waiting for us for a week down at the point. John Torres' bunch. These guys go out prepared; they have to camp out there, and they bring their food and liquor and stuff. They got so sick of waiting out there that they sent some guy to Riohacha to go and load up with supplies. He came back with four or five cases of aguardiente, which in English means firewater.

"These guys have been there for two days tanked up on aguardiente. There were five Colombians, and they had also passed the booze around to the Indians. So when we finally show up, late as hell, they are smashed. They all carry their side arms, and they're all shooting their guns in the air.

"One guy comes up to us with a bottle in one hand, motioning to all this blood on his neck. There was a hole right here. We didn't realise it was such a serious thing until we saw the exit hole as well. He's pointing at this hole with his gun and saying "bang, bang". Curtis and I are saying what shall we do with him . He's shot himself through the neck.

"Curtis said 'let's give him some Band-Aids.' So Curtis pours Aguardiente on the wound and tapes him up, and he's quite happy. He took a whole box of Band-Aids with him. We knew he was going to be dead that night - he had just lost too much blood - but he walked away happy as hell. That's how dangerous it is down there."

Andrew Barnes laughed as he told this story. Big joke. He is full of anecdotes. "You laugh about things later, but they're not funny at the time," he said. "There was this pilot, we called him Georgia Jim. His real name was James Blackburn Jr. A big burly guy. Fat. 300 lbs. Sharp as a whip. This guy could be a professor at Harvard. They were doing an air drop off Bimini one night, flying a DC 6, and they carried so much marijuana in that thing they used rollers to get it out the back.

"He's making his approach to the boats, letting them know he's going to start the race track, and they open the cargo door on the back. And then he realises he's only 50 feet off the deck instead of 500 feet. So he grabs the yoke with both hands and socks full power to it, and pulls it up hard. The only thing he heard was "Oyyyyy...." at the back, as old Jose went out the door. He'd got caught up in the rollers and went right out the door.

"They asked the people on the boats: 'did you find him?'

" 'Yeah,' they said, 'we picked him up.'

" 'Was he all right?'

" 'Nope. Dead as a door-nail.'"

Barnes laughed again. "In the early days, when we used to haul marijuana," he goes on, "Georgia Jim was heavily into that. He flew a lot of loads into Georgia. He got into a bad accident up there. He landed a DC 3 on the Coca Cola plantation just south of Atlanta. I asked him what happened. He said: 'I don't know. It was the strangest thing. My runway was 20 miles long and five miles wide, with an oak tree in the middle. And I hit the oak tree.' He did. He hit it with a wing and ground-looped the DC 3, and the prop came off right through the cockpit and almost severed his leg. He said: 'All those bastards would do was unload the pot.' And they left him there with gas pouring out of the wing and his leg half torn off. They finally got him off after all the bales had been removed, took him to a hospital, and dumped him in front of the emergency room.

"The doctors asked him what had happened. He said he had fallen off his motorcycle. About three days later he wakes up, and there's a big old Sheriff standing over him.   He said: 'Mr. Blackburn, we didn't find no motorcycle out there, but we think you might know something about that DC 3.'   He did some time in jail for that.   They gave him three months for the drug residue, and two years for criminal trespass."

CHAPTER TWELVE
Full Stop, Loaded

The laughing stopped and the last of the glamour evaporated shortly before Christmas, 1985. Barnes and Emmer were not working for Torres exclusively. In early December they had an offer from another source to haul 400 kg of cocaine from Colombia to Cat Island in the Bahamas and, of course, they accepted. This time the Cuban drug dealer for whom they were working waiting until they landed, then disappeared with the consignment without paying them a cent. "He just took off and ripped us off, and left us looking like idiots," said Barnes bitterly.

They were therefore not in a receptive mood when Torres approached them a few days later with a proposition to fly a load of cocaine into North Eleuthera. Both men refused. But Torres had his own methods of persuasion, and after Barnes' car was set alight outside his apartment he decided to see the Cuban's point of view. Anyway, it was Christmas. They needed the money. Torres assured them that the authorities on the island had all been paid off, and there would be no trouble. He lied.

Barnes and Emmer flew deep into Colombia, picked up 350 kilos of cocaine, worth an estimated $17,500,000, and flew to North Eleuthera in a Piper Navajo belonging to Julio Diaz.   They were accompanied by a Colombian "kicker", Napoleon Sanchez.

The weather was poor, with a cloud-base of less than 800 feet, when they neared the Bahamas.   In order to get their bearings they were forced to fly to Nassau, using the island's radio location beacon, and pick up an outbound radial beam on the VOR to take them to their destination. It was 2 o'clock in the morning and pitch dark, but Barnes was   uncomfortable at passing so close to civilisation. He was sure they would be spotted.

"The gig is up," he said to Emmer.   And it was.

Torres was supposed to be waiting for them at the airstrip, but there was no reply from his portable VHF radio.   Still, at least the strip was lit.   The main beams from two parked cars sprang into life and illuminated the runway threshold as they circled, trying to decide whether it was safe to land. There were other cars there, too. Too many, thought Barnes. He was nervous.   But with the fuel tanks on the Navajo almost empty they had nowhere else to go.

"We didn't like landing without talking, but we didn't have a whole lot of choice," said Barnes.   "We had to get this bird down.   We came screaming in over the top of the Jeeps and landed, and they followed us down the runway. It turned out that it wasn't John Torres at all - they were Bahamian cops."

North Eleuthera was a busy island that night.   As the three men jumped from the aircraft and did their best to disappear into the night, they heard gunfire at the other end of the runway. The police were not firing at them, but at a rival group of Bahamian smugglers who were intent on stealing the load of drugs.

It was a welcome diversion. Barnes and his colleagues thought they had made their escape, but then a police helicopter appeared and hovered over them, its floodlights pinning them against the tarmac. To make matters worse Curtis Emmer, who had suffered previous injuries to his legs, was so stiff from the long flight that he could hardly walk, let alone run.

"We are trying to run and he keeps falling over, and we keep going back to pick him up," Barnes recalled. "And then all of a sudden they started firing at us with shotguns. They hit Curtis in the leg, and that was it. We just lay down and they arrested us."

Torres was actually at the airport while this was going on, hiding in a ditch. He had left his portable radio, with which he could have warned the crew of the ambush, in his pick-up truck where it was later discovered.

The Cuban escaped by accosting a courting couple in a car near the airport and bribing them to drive him to safety. It transpired, according to Barnes, that his scheme had been to tip off the authorities, allow the cocaine to be confiscated, and then buy it back from the police. In that way he could effectively rip off the load without its Colombian owners realising he had done so. He could claim to be the innocent victim of police efficiency as far as the Colombians were concerned. If they knew the truth, they would kill him.

At that moment, Barnes and Emmer were not too kindly disposed towards Torres, either. They were on their way to Her Majesty's Foxhill Prison, Nassau. It was not a nice place.

Foxhill Prison is a relic of the British colonial era in the Bahamas. It was built on the theory, then current in the British penal system, that in order to punish a man it is not sufficient to deprive him of his liberty - you must also degrade him. There are no toilet basins in the cells, only buckets in which to urinate and defecate, and the prisoners must go through the quaint morning ritual of "slopping out." The place stinks of human excrement. There are 1,200 prisoners crammed into a building designed to house 250.

As drug smugglers, Barnes and Emmer were automatically placed in the maximum security wing of the prison. Their cell, a cement-floored dungeon with no bunks, no daylight, and only a single blanket for warmth, was shared with a number of Haitians and Rastafarians. "A freaky bunch who never washed," said Barnes. "The prison authorities try to wear you down. It also gives you an incentive to pay them to let you out, but the more money you give them, the longer they will keep you in Nassau, until you're broke. Then they would let you out."

It was here that Andrew Barnes was brought face to face with the true significance of what he had been doing. The knowledge did little to curb his smuggling activities after he was released, but at least he could no longer pretend that he was carrying an innocent recreational drug for the benefit of wealthy lawyers and doctors. Virtually every other prisoner in Foxhill was a cocaine addict.

Said Barnes: "All you hear is screaming. It's like a chimpanzee cage at night. Those are the coke addicts trying to dry out. I watched these people climb the walls when they couldn't get the stuff. They literally went berserk for about a week. In fact there's a good chance that you'll die during that week, and I guess a lot of them do die, because you see the meat wagon come around and they drag the guy down the hallway."

It might have been enough to give him pause for thought about what he was doing. But of course, once he was out of prison, Andrew Barnes could no longer hear the screams. Barbara Barnes, quickly alerted to her husband's plight, was horrified to learn that he probably faced four years or more in this hell-hole. There was no question of his guilt; he had been caught red-handed with more than seven hundred pounds of cocaine on board his aircraft. This was no technical offence like the Aruba incident. It was going to take more than a fast-talking lawyer to get him off this time. She hastened quickly to Nassau.

It seemed hopeless, but in the world of drug smuggling there are no such things as absolutes, apart from death. A few days later Barnes and Emmer had a visitor in their prison cell: his name was Arlington Butler. Arlington Butler was a prominent Nassau lawyer, and a good friend of Nigel Bowe. Like Bowe he was extremely rich and had every intention of becoming richer. He told Barnes and Emmer that he could arrange for one of them to be released. For a price, of course. They could decide between themselves who the lucky man was going to be.

The smugglers were not wholly surprised. It was common knowledge that such things went on in the Bahamas. "If two pilots go into Foxhill, they want one out to pay for the other one to get out," Barnes explained. "It's the only way they make any money. If they are convinced that nobody will help you out, as soon as you run out of money they let you out of jail there. It's a funny system."

The two men talked, and decided that Emmer should be the one to stay in jail, on the understanding that Barnes would make every effort to buy his freedom in turn. To make the deal seem more plausible when they appeared in court, it was agreed that they would exchange roles and swear that Emmer was the pilot and Barnes only the co-pilot.

The Englishman had funds stashed away in a Freeport bank, and Barbara was instructed to take the first installment of $20,000 to Wilbert Moss, an attorney who was a close associate of Arlington Butler.   She brought it to his home, where he stuffed it into an empty cornflakes packet.

"I said, 'tell your kids not to have cornflakes for breakfast,'" she recalled.   "It was really strange."

Altogether, before Andrew Barnes appeared before Nassau Magistrates Court, the couple paid over $50,000 to Arlington Butler.   It was all the money they had in the Bahamas, and the lawyer probably knew it.   At all events, the two men were promptly arraigned before magistrate Sharon Wilson, and Barnes was duly (if inexplicably) acquitted.   He had been in Foxhill Prison for two months. Curtis Emmer was destined to remain there for a further two years.

"They just arrange the trial over there," said Barnes. "It's all a spoof, really.   It's just made to look fairly legitimate.   They're really good at shaking people down. They draw it out, so that they get some here and some there, and some more and some more."

According to the unwritten rules of the game, the dealer who organised the smuggling trip, and was making the most profit, should have been responsible for incidental expenses.   These would normally include pay-offs to police, customs officials and airport staff, plus any fines or payments to spring pilots from jail.   John Torres, however, refused to play.   He told Barbara Barnes bluntly that Andrew and Curtis Emmer must solve their own problems; that "we all take a risk in this business."   He declined to hand over any money, either to her or to Mrs. Emmer.

"He just flat abandoned us," said Barnes bitterly.

Torres was visited at his home in Florida by T. Langton Hilton, another rich Bahamian lawyer closely connected to Prime Minister Sir Lynden Pindling. Hilton told the Cuban that he could arrange for Emmer's release, for a price. The method was simple: by arrangement with Donald Scott, the Bahamas' Prison Commissioner, any foreigner could be smuggled out of jail. He would still be listed as a prisoner; he would simply not be in the prison. If there were any inquiries, the story would be that the offender had been taken to the U.S. for hospital treatment.

There was nothing unusual about Hilton's approach to Torres. After every big drug bust, Bahamian attorneys would seek out the men known to be behind the shipment with similar offers. It was a new refinement of the hallowed legal practice of "ambulance chasing."

But Torres would have none of it. For all he cared, Curtis Emmer could stay in prison until he rotted. He was only a pilot, after all. There were plenty more where he came from. It was a decision he would live to regret, for Andrew Barnes was now an angry and vengeful man.

For the moment, however, Barnes decided to postpone his moment of revenge. He needed money to buy Emmer's release, and so, incredibly, he went back to work for the man who had been instrumental in getting him in jail and leaving him there.

The base of operations was now moved to Providenciales, a small island in the Turks and Caicos group. There, Barnes rented a luxurious house for a year and moved in with his whole family. He still had some money left after bribing his way out of Foxhill Prison, and reckoned he was too "hot" to live in the U.S. any more. Barbara Barnes had sold the house in Coral Springs. The grand plan was that he should work hard at the smuggling game for a year, at the end of which time he would have enough money to free Curtis Emmer, and enough left over to move anywhere in the world and start afresh. It was a triumph of hope over experience.

For a start, Torres continued to pay far less than he promised, frequently claiming that the bales of marijuana dropped off Puerto Rico had been broken up or confiscated. The wonder is that Barnes should ever have expected it would be otherwise.

Most of the money that was paid, according to Barnes, found its way to Curtis Emmer's release fund via a lawyer called Ariel Missik in Grand Turk, who was supposed to pass it to a Bahamian attorney named Godfrey Pinder. Emmer, however, remained in jail. Torres still refused to help.

"He had the money," said Barnes. "It wouldn't have cost much to get Curtis out. He just had to give $50,000 to T. Langton Hilton, and Curtis could have come on back.   But Torres would never do it.   I confronted him one time and said: 'Don't pay me - go and get Curtis out. I'll still be broke, poor and pitiful down here, and I'll have to fly your next trip.   I thought it would work that way, but I never got through to him."

Apart from Torres' obduracy, there appear to have been two main reasons for Emmer's continued incarceration.   In the first place, Barnes was paying-off the wrong people.   In the second, the market had been ruined by the action of a group of Colombian drug dealers, who paid $800,000 dollars to gain the freedom of two pilots subsequent to Barnes' release.

This made the Bahamians think, very understandably, that they had been letting prisoners go too cheaply. They locked the cell doors firmly on those who remained, in the hope that more largesse would be forthcoming.

"They thought fifty or a hundred grand was a joke," said Barnes.   After a while, he gave up.   Between them, he and another friend of Emmer's had contributed $125,000 in bribes without any result.

Ultimately, Curtis Emmer solved his own problem: he went on hunger strike, reducing his weight from 190 lb. to 119 lb. and becoming severely ill.   This made it more trouble than it was worth to keep him in jail, and he was shipped back to the United States - where he was promptly re-arrested.

For Curtis Emmer this was a remarkable stroke of luck. Had he been an honest man, under no indictment, he would have had to pay for his own medical treatment. Ill as he was, and having no money, and no health insurance, he would probably have died. In the event he was nursed back to health at the taxpayer's expense, ready to start a new prison sentence in far more congenial circumstances. America is a strange and wonderful place.

Meanwhile, Andrew Barnes was living a fairly pleasant existence in Providenciales. There were bars, and restaurants and roads, and even a school for Andy Jr. It was a better place to be than the island of South Caicos, sixty miles away, from which he conducted his smuggling activities. Barnes describes South Caicos as "a terrible place; thoroughly evil."

"On South Caicos," he said, "they would rip you off and cut your head off if they could. Every black there was into ripping everybody off."

By this time he had a new co-pilot, Chuck Portis, whom he had met while in jail in Nassau. Portis had just been released after serving 18 months of a three-year term for being caught with a load of cocaine on North Eleuthera on only his very first smuggling trip. He, too, had left a colleague behind in Foxhill Prison. Neither had had the funds to bribe their way to freedom.

Portis had served with the US Air Force in England as a loadmaster on giant C5A transport aircraft. But he was also a private pilot with his commercial and multi-engine ratings, which he had gained with an Air Force flying club.   He and Barnes had discussed the idea of working together while still in prison, with a view to freeing both their co-pilots, but Portis went back to Georgia after his release and it was a month before the Englishman heard from him.

Finally, he turned up on Providenciales.   Barnes told him the situation was less promising than he had hoped. "The only thing I've managed to scrape up in the month I've been down here," he said,   "is the same god-damned people I've been working for before.   The other idiots coming round here don't have any front money, and they're asking you to do stupid things like landing full-stop loaded."

Landing "full-stop loaded," was exactly what had put both men in jail.   They were understandably opposed to the idea.   "We were heavily into no more full-stop landings," said Barnes.   "Everybody in Foxhill Jail was in there because they had landed close to Nassau, full-stop, with cocaine in the middle of the night.   Boom.   You land there, and there's the helicopter right on top of you. These guys have got night vision goggles, and nothing is going to get away from them.   We wanted to throw it out over the water to a boat, and that's it."

The two men agreed to work together on that basis, and promptly acquired an aircraft of their own.   Well, not legally their own, but in these circles possession was rather more than nine parts of the law.   The plane, a twin-engined Beechcraft, had been the one Barnes flew for John Torres. When Torres refused to pay what he owed, Barnes simply took it. Now they flew on behalf of another Cuban drug dealer, Marco Rodriguez.

From the point of view of paying his pilots, Rodriguez does not appear to have been much of an improvement on his predecessor. But the smuggling operation itself, between April and September of 1986, had now settled down into a comfortable routine:

"Chuck and I would leave Providenciales in the twin Beech and fly the aeroplane over to South Caicos, where we had it all paid off. We were bribing the ramp supervisor, Loftin Thomas. We called him Red. We would pay him $2,000 as a deposit, and he would arrange for his guy to be in the control tower.

"Thomas ran the ramp over there. He was in charge of unloading the baggage and the cargo at South Caicos International. Just the chief coon on the ramp. He would have his guy in the tower when we departed so that the flight plan would be held - it would not be put in the computer or on the teletype. It would look like we just made a local test flight when we came back the next day, as opposed to clearing out and going to Colombia and back. Thomas made a lot of money."

He did not, however, live to enjoy it. Barnes tells the story of Loftin Thomas's demise with ghoulish relish. "After I had finished my dealings with him," he said, "I heard he ripped some Cubans off and went back to Miami. Loftin was dismantled in Florida, and they mailed him back to South Caicos in different shipping crates. His upper body came in on Turks Air, and then about a week the island suppliers brought the other crate. The customs pried it open, and they said, 'oh, there's more parts of Loftin in here' His ears, though, came in an envelope."

Until he met his disjointed end, Loftin Thomas served the smugglers well. "We had it all set up there real nice," Barnes recalled. "We would leave Providenciales early in the morning, go to South Caicos, fuel up there with a full 400 gallons, and leave around noon time to be in Colombia just about dark.

"We did five trips like that, flying over Haiti, climbing to an initial altitude of 12,500 feet to get over the mountains, and then descending on the other side to get down in more comfortable air. On that route you have to get to a safe altitude because there are peaks going to 11,000 feet. We would have a heading of 180 to the Colombia peninsula, and take a ten degree whack because of the trade winds."

All these flights were made to the notorious Lighthouse strip, with its impromptu cemetery. Barnes boasts that after more than six hours in the air, with no navigational aids, he was never more than 20 miles out in his landfall.

Once there, he would call up the Colombian ground crew on his portable radio transmitter, using the code name "Blanca." Because the low angle of the sun made it difficult to line up for landing on the primitive strip, it was necessary for them to run up and down in a jeep and raise a plume of dust to give the pilots something to aim at. Then Barnes would taxi back and line the aircraft up.

"That was the crucial thing," he said. "A lot of pilots got killed because they were so happy to get there that they would just park the aeroplane in a haphazard manner and never line it up. I took great pains to do it precisely, even if it took me five times. Because once it gets dark down there, that's it. And the way those Colombians are, they'll light up anything. They'll have you running over hills. They would wait until it was good and dark, and then bring out the fuel in 55-gallon drums. It would have to be pumped in manually. It used to be quite exciting on a C.46, because you'd be up there all night. If you started fuelling around 10 o'clock you'd be done about 3 a.m. It took twenty-eight drums of fuel.

"We were carrying 2,000 lb. of pot on each trip. They would bring out 3,000 lb., and I would send back 1,000 lb. They always tried to overload the aircraft, because they get paid by the pound. You can't convince a Colombian that if the aeroplane is all burned up at the end of the strip and there are two dead pilots, he ain't going to get nothing anyway. They're willing to crapshoot on that one. Chuck was so precise that he'd even take down a pair of scales and weigh a bale, and we would order thirty of those."

The take-off from Lighthouse was timed to enable an airdrop at dawn off the tip of Andros Island. This was the difficult part, because the whole flight back over the pitch-black ocean would have to be conducted on instruments. And this particular twin-Beech had too few of those for comfort. There was no VOR or ADF navigational equipment; not even an ordinary two-way radio. There were just the standard flight instruments - a magnetic compass, the engine gauges, an artificial horizon, a turn-and-bank indicator, and a directional gyro. All the rest had been removed to make way for the long-range fuel tank, which occupied the space they had previously taken up in the nose.

"It's very important," explained Barnes, "if you are going to put 2,000 lb. in a twin Beech, and have 400 gallons of fuel, there has to be 80 gallons in the nose, just for your centre of gravity." It was that sort of attention to detail that kept him alive.

"Even then," he went on, "you're going to be taking off about 1,500 lb. over gross. You'd better be running good. You're taking off in the middle of the night. They just put out kerosene smudge pots. They would mark the end of the runway with a car, but I always told them to get it out of the way, because we would always be dragging so heavy that I would have to suck the gear up at the end of the runway.

"The strip was about 4,000 feet long. It wasn't bad, and the nice thing about it was that there was always a wind coming right into your nose at about 25 knots. I never had any trouble.

"But when you put your landing lights off it is completely dark. You are flying a heavy tail-dragger now, rotating into pitch darkness. You have an aeroplane climbing at a maximum angle of maybe one degree. Any left or right turn in the initial thirty seconds or so is going to make you cartwheel into the ground. Your wings will hit the ground, and that will be it.

"You are not accelerating. You are not climbing. It's scary. I'm an instrument instructor, but that's the thing that scared me the most. It was definitely the most deadly thing you could do. If anything went wrong with the aeroplane, that was the end. You would go right into the ocean, and those seas were running twenty feet high."

Chuck Portis did exactly that.

Portis had a problem. He had been released from jail in Nassau, but only into the custody of the FBI. He still faced charges in the United States. These arose from the fact that the aircraft with which he was caught in North Eleuthera had been rented from a fixed-base operator in Atlanta, Georgia. This was roughly equivalent to hiring the getaway car in a bank robbery from Hertz, and qualified for a charge of theft by deception.

Now he was out on bail, his brother-in-law having mortgaged his house to put up a $300,000 bond, but

Chuck Portis had no intention of standing trial again. There was no chance of being acquitted, and the likely sentence was five years imprisonment. Portis did not care for this idea. He fully intended to jump bail, and was desperately trying to earn enough money to compensate his brother-in-law for the bond which would be forfeited as a result.

Barnes claims that he did what he could to assist this noble aim. He gave Portis, he said, the lion's share of the money they earned from Rodriguez. "We were real good friends. It didn't seem unusual for me to give him $20,000 out of the pickings we got, because we knew that if we stuck together something good would come along."

But nothing good was happening yet - just a succession of ill-paid trips for Rodriguez. Ill-paid, that is, by smuggling standards. For many people, $30,000 for a day's work might sound like a fair reward. And the date of Portis's U.S. trial was coming closer.

Barnes was losing patience. "Chuck," he said, "I'm not going to fly for these people any more. They're not paying us. Let's wait until something good comes along."

Barnes could afford to do this. He had cash in hand, and his rent was paid for the next three months. He could hold on. In deciding to do so, he unwittingly signed his friend's death warrant.

Portis, on the other hand, was desperate. He was still a long way short of finding enough money to pay back his brother-in-law, and now a new possibility had emerged. His lawyer was telling him that "something could be worked out" to get him off the theft charge. But that "something" was going to cost money. A lot of money. That was why Chuck Portis, when Barnes backed away, agreed to fly a trip on his own for Marco Rodriguez.

The chosen aircraft was a Piper Navajo Chieftain with a Panther modification, giving a 400-horse power engine on each side instead of the usual 350-horse power. It was a super-performance aeroplane. Unfortunately, it did not have a super-performance pilot. Portis was very shortsighted and wore thick glasses, which made it especially difficult for him to fly at night. Nor was he accustomed to flying as pilot-in-charge, particularly under the difficult conditions encountered in taking off from the Lighthouse strip. "He was a great co-pilot and a great mechanic," said Barnes, "but in the left-hand seat he was no good at all."

Portis had, however, flown to Lighthouse in the Navajo twice before; on both occasions as co-pilot to Andrew Barnes. And Barnes had shown him how to handle the overweight take-offs, running to maximum speed and using every inch of the runway before taking off. It was not the way the book said to do it, but then the book had probably never envisioned the problems of flying loads of marijuana from a dirt runway in Colombia.

"Chuck would always tell me," said Barnes, "'we don't need that much airspeed on this aeroplane.' He'd say 100 knots. I'd say, give me 110. He'd say: 'go ahead, Andy, rotate.' I'd say, 'shut up, Chuck.' I'd wait until the end. I would almost melt the tires on the aeroplane before I committed myself. I wanted as much airspeed on that overloaded s.o.b. as I could get. We were going out of there 1,500 lb. overloaded. About 15 or 20 per cent overweight. I would just ease it off and rocket into the sky, but he always wanted to go by the book."

Barnes was in Jamaica, the night that Chuck Portis died. He had taken Barbara and the children on a short holiday to Port Antonio, chartering another twin-engined Beechcraft because his own was becoming too well known.

"The second night we were in Jamaica," he recalled, "I woke up in the middle of the night - so help me God. I believe in God. You have to believe in God when you fly where I do. I woke up in the middle of the night and said: we've lost Chuck. Barbara remembered. Chuck died that night. He went into the water. I didn't even remember it the next day."

It was four or five days later before he knew for certain that something was wrong: "I checked in with the islander sleeping in our house on Providenciales. He told me Marco had been calling a hundred times. I said: 'I ain't flying for that son of a bitch no more.' 'No, he said, it's real important. Chuck's missing. Call him.'

"I finally call him, and Marco is real sombre. He said: 'Chuck went and did a trip for me, but he never came back. I think he ripped the plane off. Have you got anything to do with this?'

"I said 'no, Marco, you sick sod. We might tear up the town once in a while, but we're not going to steal your damned aeroplane. Tell me what happened'. He said: 'I think we've lost Chuck.'"

"They'd lost 2,000 lb. of pot, and he'd lost a Navajo Chieftain. But I'd lost Chuck. We really miss Chuck. We tried to find out more, called a lot of airports....but the long and the short of it was he took off from Lighthouse, overloaded, and didn't fly an overloaded drill."

"You had to finesse it off," Barnes explained. "I used to climb that thing at 160 knots with the cowl flaps open and full power. Chuck would be starting to lean the engines out and keep the cowl flaps closed, but I just flew it like I would a heavily loaded C.46 on military procedure. He was trying to finesse it all the time, and I think he over-finessed it.

"A Navajo is very tricky on pitch control. Just a little movement makes a big difference. And when it's tail-heavy it's ten times worse. You just have to sneeze on that thing and it starts porpoising on you. It's very short-coupled. The worst moment is when you turn your landing lights off. I bring them up with the gear. All of a sudden it is pitch dark. I think he got into a dark situation like that. He realised he was climbing too steeply, shoved it down, and was too close to the water."

Andrew Barnes would never find out exactly what happened to his friend.   He gleaned what little there was to know from the Indians at Lighthouse.   "He always wanted to go by the book," he said sadly.   "I think that's what happened to him when he went down there on his own - he did it by the book.   The people on the ground could only see the exhaust contrails go into the water. They couldn't judge how far it was off the coast.   The tail of the aeroplane with the N-numbers washed ashore, and also a badly decomposed head.   That was all that was left. The beard was still on it, and Chuck was heavily bearded. They buried it right next to the airstrip, where they bury all the dead pilots and crews."

There, but for the grace of whoever looks after drug smugglers, went Andrew Barnes.   "That Navajo almost got me one night," he recalled.   "I shoved the nose down instinctively, because I got too damn slow.   Luckily we had 200 feet.   If I had been lower, where I think Chuck got into that situation, we would have gone into the water. I got it back.   I was lucky.   I got it back.   But Chuck wasn't lucky that night."

CHAPTER THIRTEEN
Invitation to Murder

Andrew Barnes had apparently changed his mind about Marco Rodriguez. At least, if he promised $100,000 for a flight, he would usually pay $40,000 or $50,000. Something, at least. Compared with John Torres, who came up with nothing but expenses and excuses, that made him the best game in town. Now Marco had a new idea: he would provide a C.46 - the same type of aircraft that Barnes had crashed off Norman's Cay - if the Englishman would fly it for him. By now Barnes had become something of a legend among the smugglers. He was better than a good pilot, he was a lucky pilot, and his luck had held for a long time. Though he had a shrewd suspicion that Rodriguez had bought the big bird with money that should have been paid to him, he agreed to the new deal.

In a single flight, the C.46 could carry seven times as much marijuana as the twin-engined Beechcraft: 14,000 lbs. of the illicit weed. This made it a more profitable proposition, especially since, now that he had lost his co-pilot, Barnes would be flying it on his own, except for a kicker in the back. He was guaranteed $100,000 for each trip. Whatever that guarantee was worth.

The mode of operation was also to be changed. Now the smugglers would be using the massive disused airstrip at Mayaguana at the southern end of the Bahamas chain for delivering the cargo from Colombia. The Mayaguana runway was 10,000 feet long, having been built by the U.S. government to support a tracking station for the Apollo space program. Though long abandoned, it was in excellent condition, and having been constructed to handle large cargo jets was more than adequate for the heavily laden C.46. To Andrew Barnes, used to squeezing in and out of jungle strips, it was a vision of heaven. His orders were to land at night, leave the aircraft until first light, and then fly to Great Inagua - a Bahamian island on the other side of the Caicos group. From there he would take the C.46 back to Providenciales on a legal flight plan.

Barnes knew Great Inagua well. The southernmost of the Bahamian chain, it lay just to the west of the British-owned Turks and Caicos Islands. He had first been there ten years previously, when there was just a little fishing village with the native inhabitants walking around bare-footed. Apart from fishing, the only available work was in the salt fields, and the only way to get from the airport to town was on foot.

Things were very different now. The people were still living in crude huts, and the roads were still full of pot-holes, but now every primitive house had a satellite television dish and a VCR, and the natives were driving BMW's with Rolex watches on their wrists. Something had happened to Great Inagua, and that something was drugs.

Nobody was fishing any more. "You can't even eat fish on Great Inagua now because nobody will go out to fish," said Barnes. "They are all out at the airport preparing to receive a load of coke. All the young people. The old people have turned their backs. The Bahamas only have 180,000 people, but I would say half of them are cocaine addicts. Everybody is stoned out on coke all the time, because they rip a lot of it off. There are a lot of suicides."

Andrew Barnes said this with concern, but without any apparent sense of guilt. He adds: "There are some islands there that just can't exist unless drug smuggling continues." Does he not realise his own responsibility for the disaster? Barnes shrugs. "Barbara and I have never been drug users, so talking about cocaine addiction goes right over my head. I don't know what it does." This, long after the experiences in Foxhill Prison; long after seeing what was happening to the Bahamas. Moral myopia is a convenient affliction.

For several weeks the arrangement went smoothly, at least as far as any interference from the law was concerned. Some twenty tons of marijuana were flown across the Caribbean to Mayaguana, with Barnes alone at the controls of the C.46. It was dangerous, especially given his drinking habits, but he contended that "I'd rather do it that way that have some of these other turkeys with me."   The police in the British-owned Turks Islands, well paid-off, chose to ignore the fact that the big aircraft in their back yard was illegal from virtually every standpoint.

Relations with Rodriguez were a different matter. The Cuban paid once - $100,000 - but that was all. Most of that money, according to Barnes, went to the abortive Curtis Emmer release fund and on bribes to various officials on the island.   It was the old story.   Barnes claims that at this point he wanted to abandon the smuggling game. "If only I could have got Curtis out," he said plaintively, "I would have stopped."   It is even possible that he believes this. But as Tom Paine wrote in The Age of Reason: "It is necessary to the happiness of man that he be mentally faithful to himself.   Infidelity does not consist in believing, or in disbelieving, it consists in professing to believe what one does not believe."   And Barnes was not happy.

At the very least he wanted to get free of Marco Rodriguez, but there were hazards in trying to change employers.   "To jump ship was dangerous," he explained, "because the next person you are dealing with could be a cop. It could be the DEA.   So you get into a kind of a mould where you just accept getting half pay for what you do. It's better to do it that way than to switch completely with a group and start all over again."

But then he found Julio Diaz again.   Or, to be more accurate, Julio Diaz found him.   Diaz was a doctor, a rich doctor, owning two clinics and two pharmacies in Miami. Most of his money, however, had come from drugs of a different kind. The two men knew each other from the Carlos Lehder days, when Diaz had supplied the penicillin to cure the outbreak of gonorrhoea on Norman's Cay. Barnes had also flown him to the island once or twice to perform bullet-extractions when things had gotten a little out of hand in Lehder's fiefdom. As a sideline, he could always be relied on to fake a pilot's medical exam, for a price.

Dr. Diaz had an intriguing proposition for Andrew Barnes, whom he had apparently forgiven for losing his Piper Navajo in the debacle on North Eleuthera. "Come to Panama," he said, "and bring the Beechcraft. I've got something really good for you. Stop flying that C.46 and come to work for me."

He would give no details, and only provided sufficient expenses to cover the 400 gallons of fuel needed for the seven-hour non-stop flight. It was a blind date. None the less, Barnes trustingly accepted the offer and flew the twin-Beechcraft he had hi-jacked from John Torres into Paitilla, a small private airport just outside the city of Panama. There he was met by Diaz and a reception committee of Panamanians, one of whom was a colonel in military uniform. He was also introduced to Irvin Manzanares, owner of a company called Alas del Caribe which operated the fixed-base facilities at Paitilla. Barnes was intrigued, and encouraged. It began to look as though there was some clout behind this thing, whatever it was. Perhaps his days of risking his life with night flights into remote airstrips had come to an end.

Diaz instructed him to book into a hotel and begin to look for an apartment. He would, he said, be in Panama for several months. But he still refused to tell him any details of the plan.

"Don't worry, Andy. Don't worry," he said. "I'll let you know. You're going to be really surprised. This is very great."

The pilot protested. "Look," said Barnes, "I've read a lot about Panama. This is no place in the world to be fooling around. These guys take things seriously down here, especially with drugs. The prisons are bad - I've heard you can't buy your way out of them."

"Oh no," said Diaz. "You've got it wrong. This guy Manzanares works right with Noriega, and everything we do down here is taken care of. It's protected, completely protected. Don't worry, we've got all this covered here."

And so it seemed, at first. Barnes found himself installed in a luxurious high-rise flat on Panama's Via Argentina, and given a car to use whenever he wanted. He began to think seriously of moving Barbara and the children from Providenciales to Panama. As for the work, it was not only easy, it was legal. He spent his days flying cargoes of crabs and lobsters to various parts of Panama - to Changuinola, David, Contadora Island and Las Perlas Island - just so that the authorities would get used to the sight of the Beechcraft.   For this, Barnes was being paid a salary of $3,000 a month.

By his standards this was not much money.   But he knew, of course, that his current spell of honest employment was no more than a cover for what was to come.   Diaz had at last confided to him that what was in store was a "mother-lode" of cocaine.

The cash register in Andrew Barnes' imagination began to click again with the prospect of making enough cash to take him to Australia, England, or anywhere else in the world where the law had not heard of him.   His self-delusion knew no limit.

There was not long to wait.   "One day," he said, "they say, 'Look, Andy, this is what the deal is: we just lost a pilot and a crew.   They got arrested up in Costa Rica in San Jose.   They're in jail.   They lost the plane and everything. Forget it; they've gone.   What we need is you and your plane.   That's why we've had you down here all this time. We want everybody to see you flying produce around; you've got a job with Alas del Caribe; you're wearing a captain's uniform.   But once a week we want you to fly just a hundred and fifty miles over here to Turbo, Colombia, and pick up 500 kg of cocaine.   It will be a manifested trip.   It won't reflect Colombia.' They wanted me to fly the plane to the San Blas Islands on the north side of Panama, and instead of landing there go on to Turbo, load up, and bring the cocaine to Changuinola in Panama."

Barnes hardly paused for thought: "I said: 'That's great.' I had been to Changuinola, it's a military airport. Everything would be completely paid for, and I would be working for Noriega, the strong man in Panama. So I said: 'Yeah, I'll do it.'

But I'm smart enough not to bring my wife and kids down there. I said: 'look, I want to get a couple of these jobs done before I mix my family up in this.'

"So I'm slated to do a trip within two days. They're happy because I agreed to do it. They just told me to stay in my apartment for a couple of days, and not to go out and get blasted."

Andrew Barnes did as he was told. He stayed in his apartment and did not get drunk. At least, not more than normally drunk. But his re-birth as a Noriegan employee was destined to be aborted.

"About two days go by," he recalled, "and I hear that Noriega's personal pilot has been murdered down in Colombia. I asked Julio and Manzanares what that meant. There was a lot of publicity about it. They said: 'Don't worry about it. There's nothing to worry about.' What had happened was that there was some confusion about a load. Noriega had taken a load from the cartel and ripped them off. It was 500 kg of cocaine that he said had been stolen from him. When they sent the pilot back down to Colombia to pick up another load, the Medellin Cartel people just blew him away and kept the aeroplane."

For Andrew Barnes, who was uncomfortably aware that that pilot could have been him, the news came like a cold douche.   His new environment was not the safe and cosy place it seemed.   He was playing with the big boys now, and the big boys played rough.

"I don't like this," he told Diaz.   "They're playing dirty games here."

He was arrested the same day.   The police came to the apartment and picked up Barnes, Diaz, and a man named Georgie Mendez who was to fly as co-pilot on the trips to Colombia.   They missed Manzanares.

All three men were taken to the headquarters of the G.2 section of the Panamanian police, which deals with narcotics.   Barnes was interrogated for two days. Ironically, after all the things he had done and got away with, he was now being suspected of complicity in a crime about which he knew nothing.

"The implication," he said, "was that the people I was working for had killed Noriega's pilot.   I found out later that they had intelligence reports from the DEA, linking me with Lehder.   But these reports were from way back in 1980 when I had been flying for him.   They had given this information to G.2, who figured I was still working for Lehder and the cartel, and that they had blown away Noriega's pilot.

"I denied this vehemently, because I had nothing to do with Lehder.   They kept us there for about two days, never knowing exactly what the hell was going on.   I kept screaming for the ambassador. I said: 'look, I'm British. You can beat me or kill me, but you're going to have it show up somewhere.' I raised hell.

And then, much to his surprise, Andrew Barnes was released.

"They said okay, you're going now. They took me and Diaz to the airport. Our bags and everything are all back at the apartment. They said: 'you get out of here, right now.' They ordered us out. They took me to the twin Beech, which was sitting at Paitilla already fuelled up. It was better than sitting in jail.

"I said: 'Hey, let's go.' So we pre-flight the plane and take off. The engines are running a little bit soft. I didn't have full power on take-off, and I commented to Georgie about it. But I just put it down the fact that it was real hot morning, 100 degrees, and I hadn't slept in two days. I just figured it was me feeling bad, and not the aeroplane.

"We got on up to altitude. I was heading back to Providenciales, and the first leg was taking me to Kingston, Jamaica. That's about a four-hour leg. On all those long over-water segments I made a habit of getting up high. I was at about 12,500 ft, and it took me a long time to get up there. I am saying to Georgie: 'this plane feels likes its carrying lead weights in the belly.' It felt like a grossed-out twin Beech, and it was empty.

"Leaving Panama you head north over the isthmus. At 60 miles you cross over Colon, and from there you are heading out over open ocean. I was 60 miles over the ocean when I leveled off at 12,500 feet. I settled down, started leaning the aeroplane out, and the right engine went 'bang,bang,bang' about three times, and quit. I'm selecting fuel tanks, and I've got the boost pumps on, because I think I've got a fuel interruption. I push my mixtures all the way forward. I'm trying everything I can. I figure we're out of fuel. But all the tanks are full; I've just checked them.

"I'm doing everything I can, but I just cannot get that engine started. I wind up having to feather it. I said: 'Jesus Christ, this is all we need, Georgie.' There is no other place to turn to but back to Panama. I'm not heading out over three more hours of open ocean to Kingston with a dead engine on one side.

"So I resign myself to going back to Panama. I've had engine failures before. It was no big deal. But we do take the precaution of putting our life jackets on and getting the raft out, so if things did occur in a hurry we'd be in a position to ditch.

"I put a Mayday distress call out. I got an Air Panama jet going into Panama that acknowledged it, and relayed the information that we were turning round and that our status was questionable, but we were holding our own.

"Five minutes later, the left engine starts to do the same thing. First of all, it backfired a couple of times and ran rough. Looking at the engine, it was just shaking in its cradle out there. But this one isn't quite dead. I am saying to myself 'Christ Almighty, what the hell is going on here ?' It took me ten minutes - I had to make sure that I hadn't screwed up; that I hadn't turned the fuel off, or something stupid like that. But I couldn't find anything wrong with the plane. It was all in normal running configuration. I thought maybe I was dreaming and had turned the mags off accidentally. No. Nothing. The left engine would run, backfire, and then die. It kept surging like that. But there was enough power, not to sustain altitude but to flatten the glide. So much so that when we got to the coastline at Colon we still had 6,000 feet of air underneath us.

"Our decision was not to go to another airport in Panama, and perhaps really get into trouble, but to try to make Paitilla and explain what has been going on.

"At this point in time I had no idea what was wrong. I was just trying to get that sick bird down in one piece. But that engine hangs in there, backfiring and missing and skipping, but it's running. And we put the aeroplane down in Paitilla.

"No sooner do we land than we are surrounded by G.2 again. I said: 'Hi, guys, we're back.'"

The Panamanians were surprised to see him, and a little disconcerted. "We threw you out of the country," they said. "Why have you come back?"

The party were taken down town for another four-hour interrogation by narcotics agents, before being put on a commercial flight to Haiti later in the day. Barnes was told frankly that his aircraft had been sabotaged; that he had never been intended to make it across the Caribbean, let alone return.

"Somebody," said the men from G.2, "not us, but somebody, screwed up the magnetos.   They loosened the backing plates."

The saboteurs had done a good job on the starboard engine.   As intended, the backing plate screws had finally fallen out under the influence of vibration, causing the distributor to fall off and short out the whole magneto. On the port engine they had not been quite so thorough; the screws had remained in place just long enough for the aircraft to limp back to Panama.

The attempted assassination, said the agents, had been Noriega's response to Carlos Lehder.   "You can tell your buddies down there,"   they added, "that we don't appreciate them killing one of our pilots."

Andrew Barnes' past had come back to haunt him. But once again he had survived.   For his part, Julio Diaz is now serving a long term of imprisonment in Nassau, having been caught on a Chub Cay airstrip with a planeload of drugs.

CHAPTER FOURTEEN
Subsistence Money

In the course of his drug-smuggling career Andrew Barnes had crashed three times, been jailed twice, and had had more close calls with accidental death than a drunken trapeze artiste.   Now he had survived an assassination attempt.   Someone up there seemed to be trying to tell him something, and for once he listened.   Barnes decided that the moment had come to quit.   It was a short-lived decision, but no doubt he meant it at the time.   Anyway, he had lost the twin-engined Beechcraft, confiscated in Panama by DEA agent Douglas Driver, so his options were limited.

Although he had long been convinced that the law was waiting for him in the United States, Barnes now decided to move his family back there from Providenciales.   With them in a borrowed Beechcraft came two rabbits, the same ill-tempered chow that I met in Pennsylvania, and a toucan bird.   The law must have been looking the other way, for they gained entrance without incident, apart from a two-hour delay in customs.   There was still no indictment against him; no warrant out for his arrest.

He and Barbara moved north and negotiated to buy the Quakertown house for $130,000.   There were soon horses in the paddock and dogs in the yard, and there was lots of room for the children to play.   They were, to all outward appearances, a respectable middle-class American family of modest means. They even had a $100,000 mortgage - with repayments of $1,200 a month - though ostensibly no income with which to meet the installments.

And then the telephone began to ring. Barnes was to learn later that the FBI and the DEA were actively searching for him at this stage, but they were evidently less efficient than his old associates. John Torres and Marco Rodriguez knew exactly where he was. They called him two, three, or four times a day, demanding that he fly for them again.

"I told Barbara," he said, "to tell them I was not there. I didn't want to mess with this thing again. But they kept calling, and I finally agreed to go down to Miami to meet them."

Barnes' New Year resolution was beginning to slip. He was, of course, broke again. When Barbara told him that they were $5,000 short of the amount needed to meet the closing costs on the Pennsylvania house, it proved to be the decisive factor that drove him back to smuggling. He went to see Marco Rodriguez.

Rodriguez and Torres, who had long been bitter rivals, were now working together. They had acquired a C.46, registration No. 625CL, with which they wanted Barnes to fly marijuana from Colombia to the Bahamas. With some asperity he pointed out that when he worked for them individually, neither had paid him properly.

"Ah," Rodriguez replied, "but now we are working together we can guarantee that you will get paid."

Barnes didn't believe them, but he took the job anyway.

He needed the money. Any money. He picked up the C.46 in Miami and flew it to his old stamping ground of Providenciales. It was early 1987. Carlos Lehder had been arrested in Colombia and was facing extradition to the United States, and the U.S. authorities were finally stepping up their interdiction. Yet down in the Turks and Caicos Islands business was proceeding as normal. Drug business, that is.

"To get away with an aeroplane that size, at that late date, was incredible," said Barnes. "And then to operate it on three separate trips without any law enforcement pressure at all was weird."

Weird, but it happened. For once the flights were almost routine. They would fly to Colombia, pick up seven tons of marijuana, and return through the night to the magnificent disused American runway on Mayaguana Island. There, the drugs would be unloaded in time for a dawn take-off and the short flight to Great Inagua, where falsified legal documents would be provided to return the C.46 to South Caicos.

There were no problems. On Great Inagua the smugglers paid off Winston Burrows, who ran the fuel concession at the airport, and Cleveland Palacious, a local businessman who owned Tops Bar, their favourite watering hole.   Both were black Bahamians.   Palacious and Burrows in turn paid off the Customs and police authorities; so well, in fact, that Barnes' aircraft, covered with the red dust of Colombia, was washed off after each flight by a police sergeant and two corporals.

Once back on South Caicos, having ostensibly completed a simple legal flight around the islands - a fiction that no one believed for a moment - the smugglers would relax at the Admiral's Arms hotel and wait for news of the fishing boats that were carrying the marijuana to Nassau.   From there the load would be transferred into the fast speedboats that would make the final run into Florida.   If they failed to make it, Barnes would not get paid.

"There were lots of excuses," he said.   "They sank, they ran into each other, they got ripped off, they got busted.   I got to the point where I thought that every time a boat went out, it sank.   I have never yet seen a boat go out of Florida and make it back without being pirated or shot at or busted or sunk, or something."

All the same, he did get some money.   Not as much as he had been promised, naturally.   But then that was par for the course with Torres and Rodriguez.   In all, Barnes received $60,000 for his three trips in the C.46 over a short period.

It was not enough; certainly not enough for Barbara. She described it to me as: "Pitiful.   Subsistence-type money."

However, it came in handy: she used it to buy a turbo-charged Ford Thunderbird.

That car was not easily earned, despite the greasing of palms that kept the law at a safe distance.   625 Charlie Lima, as Barnes calls the Torres/Rodriguez C.46, was a pretty basic aeroplane.   It had no autopilot, which meant that he had to fly it manually, on instruments all the way, and there was the small matter of an aged engine on the right wing that used five gallons of oil every hour.

This meant that once they reached Colombia, Barnes would have to clamber on to the wing, twenty feet from the ground in the windblown darkness, and pour in thirty gallons of fresh oil. It was a hazardous business.

There was no co-pilot.   In a legal sense, not that anyone cared, there was no one on board entitled to fly the C.46.   Barnes' type-rating certificate, gained in the Dominican Republic, had long since expired, and the right hand seat in the cockpit on all three flights was occupied by John Torres.

Torres was not qualified to fly a kite, let alone a C.46, and his presence led to an interesting atmosphere on board.   Andrew Barnes is a placid soul, an easy-going hulk of a man, but after the incident on Nassau when Curtis Emmer was left to rot, he hated Torres with cold loathing.   Now he was condemned to sit beside him for six hours at a stretch.   To this day he has no rational explanation of why he did it.

Except money.

He said: "There were lots of times when I wanted to throw him out of there."

"He considered it," said Barbara.   "He sat back and bided his time and went along with it, never being nasty, never cussing him out.   Nothing.   But when the time was right, vengeance is mine."

"I was waiting for my time," said Andy.   But the time was not yet.   First, there was money to be made.

It was not as though Torres was of any practical use. If anything went wrong, there was no question of saying "hey, John, hold the wheel for a minute."   "Come hell or high water," said Barnes, "it was all on me.   Much as I like flying a C.46, I don't like flying in those circumstances in the middle of the night on my own. You like to talk things over, even if you're crashing.   I couldn't even do that.   I just had to sit there and spew myself."

The C.46 did have something going for it: "It flies like a ship, and when you steer it, it behaves like a ship.   It's very stable in the air, but that stability hurts you if you get screwed up."

In the small hours of the morning, on a windy day in March, Andrew Barnes duly got screwed up.   It was not wholly his fault.   The ground crew at Mayaguana, which was in total darkness because the island generators are turned off when the more honest inhabitants go to bed, had only put out a single row of paraffin lamps on the runway.   There should have been two - one on each side - to enable the pilot to line up his final approach.

With one line of lights, and no other navigational guidance, Barnes had no way of telling whether they were on one side of the strip or the other.   In fact they were laid, quite logically, in the centre.   But after a six-hour flight with the usual heavy intake of booze, the Englishman's mind was not working too swiftly.

"There was a gusting cross-wind blowing from the south east right across the runway," he recalled. "I made my turn from downwind into base just a little bit too close into the runway, and overshot my roll-out into final.   I was trying to horse this monster around and keep the speed up, because I was heavily laden with 14,000 lb. of pot in the cabin.   I got it up on one wingtip, and then realised I was only a hundred feet off the deck.   I was hitting trees with my right wingtip, lining up on final."

To some extent the error may have been caused by the variation in altimeter reading between Colombia and the Bahamas.   A legal aircraft flying into a regular airport is always given an up-to-date altimeter setting, known as a QNH, by the air traffic controller.   There were no such facilities at Mayaguana, or any other drug-smuggling strip. Most of the smuggling aircraft were fitted with a radar altimeter, which is not dependent on atmospheric pressure, to compensate for this lack.

Torres, however, had apparently decided not to waste his money on such luxuries for the C.46. Barnes was left to trust to luck and experience, and this time they had let him down. It was a dangerous situation. Now the very stability of the C.46 was its worst enemy, fighting the pilot as he wrestled with the wheel to level the wings. Fortunately the strip was long, for there was no question of going around again. "When you start going around at night-time you are screwing yourself up instrument-wise," Barnes explained. "I had all my landing lights on now, and the cockpit lights were lit up. I always like to get it on the ground the first time. I got it straightened up and did a greased-on landing. It was another instance when I've got so close to death and walked away from it. I've come so damn close, I don't know what saves me. You don't think about it that day, but later it starts clicking up."

Torres appears to have been less sanguine about the incident. All of a sudden, the C.46 operation into Mayaguana no longer seemed such a good idea. Anyway, there were bigger profits to be made from cocaine, which could be smuggled in a smaller aircraft. He and Rodriguez bought themselves a Piper Navajo, and asked Andrew Barnes to fly it. He was, after all, a very lucky pilot.

But Barnes refused, and this time stuck with his decision. It was not for moral reasons - it was a bit late for that - or even the thought that further involvement with cocaine would not be a good idea, now that Carlos Lehder was in custody and possibly singing to the feds. No, Andrew Barnes listened to his wife, who was listening to a cash register that never seemed to ring.

"I think I finally convinced you at that point," she said to him while I listened with some amusement, "that you weren't ever going to see a dime out of these people."

CHAPTER FIFTEEN
Vengeance

So Andrew Barnes went back to Pennsylvania, and there he stayed. It was a nerve-wracking period. With Carlos Lehder and Jack Carlton-Reed both under arrest - Carlton-Reed having been picked up in Panama at the time of Barnes' own escapade there - there was the constant fear of a knock on the door from the FBI. It seemed impossible to believe that Lehder would not betray his former associates in the hope of striking some deal with the federal authorities.

It was not a happy household. The drinking was getting worse; the $60,000 - the "pitiful subsistence money" - was draining away; and young Andy Jr., with approaching puberty to add to his problems, was becoming daily more difficult to handle. To try Barnes' conscience further, Curtis Emmer was still in Foxhill Prison, and starving himself to death.

And then, in September 1987, who should crawl out of the woodwork but their old friend, John Torres.

Without his favourite pilot, Torres had apparently given up on the idea of smuggling cocaine with the Navajo. He may have been unable to find anyone to fly it, for by this stage the attrition rate among smugglers was phenomenal.

"I'm one of the few guys that started ten years ago who is not in jail already, or is still alive," said Barnes.   "Most of the people I knew are dead.   Not from being blown away, or murdered; from crashes.   Just from losing it on some dark night."

But Torres, ever resourceful, had come up with a new scheme for making an illicit fortune.   He arranged to meet Barnes in Philadelphia to discuss it.   This time, he promised, there would be no perilous night flights into remote and dangerous airstrips.   It would just be a simple matter of flying, or even driving, from Miami to Philadelphia.   Torres claimed to have forged a link with the Manny Gambino mob in Philadelphia, who had commissioned him to produce artificial heroin, and a second substance called P2P, which is the principal ingredient of the popular street drug, Quaaludes.   He already had, he said, a chemist in Miami who could make the stuff. He needed Barnes to transport it.

Andrew Barnes tells two different versions of what happened next.   In the first he portrays himself as a repentant smuggler, already determined to give himself up to the FBI, to take his punishment and start a new life.   In this account, the prospect of getting involved with heroin finally tips the scale.

He said: "That was really the last thing.   I knew that if I'd gone ahead with that, even if I'd made some money....I didn't want anything to do with heroin.   Dropping pot in the water is one thing, but doing heavy stuff like that just went against my grain. And I knew if I let John go ahead with that it was bound to come back to haunt me.

"It was my intention all along to contact the FBI because I knew the handwriting was on the wall. Carlos Lehder was going to get me into trouble because he was back here. So I set John Torres up on this thing and told him to go ahead. When he came up here with the samples, that's when I contacted the FBI. I figured I would be doing myself good, and I would be getting this creep off the street."

There was also, of course, the small matter of revenge: "I had to set him up," said Barnes. "I was paying him back for leaving Curtis over there to die, and for all those flights that I had done and he hadn't paid me. He let me down on everything I had ever done for him. He left Curtis over there to die. He knew how to get him out, but he didn't want Curtis back on the street because he figured that then I wouldn't work for him any more. That's how he got about three more trips out of me than I was prepared to do. He knew I was hurting on getting Curtis out.

"So when I went into the FBI I went in with John Torres strapped around me. And that's helped me a lot. But that wasn't the reason for it: I wanted to make John think twice before he left somebody in jail.

"That last episode in jail in Nassau cost me everything - the house I had in Florida. It made me so hot that I was bound to get arrested sooner or later. Before that I was relatively cool. All the stuff with Lehder, we never even came close to getting bitten. We got a little bit of heat when that C46 went down, but there was nothing like getting busted with the stuff to make you hot."

Barbara Barnes recalled that day: "I was really scared," she said. "I went completely cold. I was like ice. We had talked about it for a couple of weeks, but actually doing it was different. One morning he just came out here and picked up the 'phone without saying a word to me. I was ice cold and completely numb, but so happy."

Even on this reading, the overall picture is hardly attractive. The role of informant, grass, or snitch, rarely is. But at least, according to this account, it was not only the twin desires of self-preservation and revenge that sent Barnes to the FBI. There was also the moral revulsion at involvement in heroin trafficking that tipped him over the edge. He ought to get some brownie points for that.

But somehow, as I transcribed this section of the interview and listened to the voices again, I sensed that this version of events did not ring true. For sure, it fitted the image of the newly-contrite Andrew Barnes to whom I had now been talking for several weeks. But it was greatly at odds with his past behaviour. After all, he had already gone back to work for Torres twice, knowing what the man was. What had been so different on this occasion?

I had the feeling, too, that Barbara Barnes might not have been so keen on the idea of her husband surrendering to the law as she now appeared. But I was not enthused with the idea of calling her a liar to her face. The lady had claws.

It was not a crucial point, but it bothered me. I decided to get Andrew on his own, and the ideal location seemed to be a sailboat that I kept on the Chesapeake Bay. It was only after he accepted the arrangement that I remembered that my smuggler-friend had never had to surrender his passport. What if he hi-jacked the boat, which was quite capable of an ocean voyage, and decided to escape jail by sailing off into the wide blue yonder? He was, after all, a great deal bigger than I was.

Luckily my fears were groundless. I don't know whether the thought occurred to him, but if it did he did nothing about it. After a pleasant sail we dropped anchor off the little Maryland town of Oxford, and I switched on the tape recorder.

"Okay, Andrew," I said. "Now tell me what really happened."

Andrew grinned, sheepishly. "I was screwing around with John Torres," he admitted. "He came up to Philadelphia with a sample of this P2P. To my mind I was still under the impression that I could make enough money to get out of this mess.

"Carlos was in jail now in the U.S. His trial was under way. I figured right then that I had six months to make some money and get out of there. I thought I would start a new life in Australia or South Africa - or somewhere where they wouldn't be looking for me.

"I thought I could still get out of there, and John Torres started the same crap. This P2P was supposed to make some money. He came up there with a couple of samples. One time he got paid $80,000 and gave me $2,000. He came up another time with four gallons of the stuff and didn't even call me. He just circumvented me completely.

"So I told Barbara, I said.....They are talking about synthetic heroin, synthetic cocaine, and the real heroin. Most of it was going to go to Puerto Rico. He was going to get it out of New York to send to Puerto Rico. I am up to my eyeballs now with John with this P2P and heroin and stuff like that.

"We hadn't done anything, but I knew he was going to cut me out of the whole thing. He was just using me because I happened to live close to Philadelphia and could pick him up from the airport.

"So one morning I'm feeling pretty sick with myself, and I'm wanting to get this thing over with. I'm almost begging to get busted. To get some help. I wake up one morning and get out of the shower and go to the phone. Barbara asks me who I'm calling. I said: 'I'm calling the FBI.'

"She said: 'about what?'

"I said: 'I'm going to turn John in and try to make a deal for myself on the Carlos thing. I just can't keep going like this.'

"I'm trying to run from one thing and make some money, and this guy's still trying to fuck me. I'm down on my knees and he's kicking me in the balls.

"I said: 'I'm going to get busted for the Carlos Lehder thing, Barbara. You know that. It might not happen this week, it might not happen this month. But without any money I'm sitting here dead in the water, and a damn U-boat's coming at me.

'I'm not going to let John get me into a situation, because you know he's going to get busted too. As soon as I get clear of all the Lehder stuff, I'm going to come out five years later and there's going to be an indictment for all the John Torres stuff. I might as well take care of all this right now.'

"It was just a shot in the dark. I didn't know what the consequences or the results would be, but I took the shot. I picked up the phone and called the FBI in Philadelphia. I said: 'I've got something I'd like to talk to you about.'"

Something else had happened to concentrate Andrew Barnes' mind, though he did not mention it in that interview. He had read in the Miami Herald that Richard Blankenship had been arrested, and had talked. From that moment on, he knew his days of freedom were numbered.

Whatever the reason, he made the call.

The FBI were happy.   Although the Bureau knew a great deal about Barnes' activities at this stage, they had apparently made no especial effort to locate him, let alone arrest him.   Indeed, when he made that first telephone call, they were inclined to regard him as a crackpot. Perhaps they were unused to drug smugglers giving themselves up, for whatever reason.

"They treated it as a joke first of all," said Barnes. "They said: 'Yeah, we get a lot of calls like this'.   I told them to meet me at my local pub, and they sent out two agents who I thought were idiots: Phil Akens and John Dragon.   They still seemed to think it was a joke or something.

"I told them there was this guy in Philadelphia, and I would be seeing him tonight.   It was up to them.   If they wanted to pick up on it, they could.   John Torres wanted me to pick him up from the Holiday Inn on Cityline Avenue in Philadelphia, where he was staying that night. I said: 'you can listen in on it if you want, and see whether I'm crazy or not.'"

At this stage Barnes had not bothered to tell the local FBI agents exactly who he was.   Perhaps it slipped his mind in his determination to incriminate John Torres. "That was going to be my next move," he said.   "I wanted to get them in a posture where they couldn't say no to this, and I could get a better deal for myself.   Actually it didn't work out that way at all, but that was what I had in my mind: they couldn't let go of this heroin deal and the

P2P. They didn't dare do that and get me hung over Lehder."

Idiots or not, Akens and Dragon accepted Barnes' offer and arranged to meet him at another hotel shortly before his scheduled meeting with the Cuban. There, the pilot was fitted with a concealed microphone and tape recorder.

Torres was completely unsuspecting. "I just let John ramble on for about an hour about what we were going to do," said Barnes. "About how we were going to bring this crap up. I didn't lead him; I just said: 'what do you want me to do? What's my part in this?'

He said: 'you are going to drive the heroin...this is how much you'll get'....he just rambled on. At the end of that conversation they didn't bust John. They analysed the tape, and after a day or two they called me up and said: 'Mr. Barnes, would you like to meet us at this hotel?' They'd checked everything out.

"And they said: 'By the way, you're quite an infamous character. We've checked you out, too.'

"They were real formal and quite polite. They said: 'We're really interested in this thing, and, by the way, there are some guys down in Jacksonville who'd like to talk to you.' I said: 'I was going to come to that.'"

It was a curious turn of events. From a fugitive felon, hiding out in the backwoods of Pennsylvania, Andrew Barnes had been transformed overnight into a minor celebrity in the eyes of the FBI. A champion of law and order, yet.   He was not slow to take advantage of the situation:

"I said: 'what's the deal. I'm not going to spill my guts until I know whether I can cut a deal or not.'"

And so, as befitted his new star status, he was flown in a chartered government jet to Jacksonville, Florida, where he met with Robert Merkle and Ernst D. Mueller, Federal Prosecutors in the Carlos Lehder case.

Although no plea-bargaining deal was worked out at this meeting, Barnes   returned to Pennsylvania, still a free man, with every reason to hope that one would soon be forthcoming.

"They told the FBI in Philadelphia," he recalled, "'this man has regional, national, and international ramifications on this problem we are trying to solve here, so we are going to work with him.'"   It made Andrew Barnes, smuggler, sound like a personage worthy of respect.

And in truth, he was in great demand.   The FBI needed his continuing services to help them catch Torres, and perhaps lead them into the centre of organised crime in Philadelphia.   The DEA were anxious to hear about his involvement with Carlos Lehder, for in all the Colombian's nefarious activities he had only once set foot in the U.S. with a load of cocaine.   And Andrew Barnes had been his pilot on that flight.   It was a crucial element in the prosecution case.

Barnes, in fact, was caught in the middle of a classic example of inter-agency rivalry. And he was not slow to exploit the situation. He had fully expected to be behind bars within hours of picking up the telephone. Now, instead, he was working actively for the very organizations that he had spent the previous nine years eluding. They were even paying for his services - though not very much. For the moment, the Torres affair took precedence. Through Barnes, the FBI learned that the Cuban was dealing with a man named Ricky Bressi, who in turn was dealing directly with Mafia boss Manny Gambino. (Bressi, Gambino's strong man, was subsequently arrested at Fort Lauderdale airport while carrying $3,000,000 in counterfeit currency, and was sentenced to five years imprisonment.)

The Bureau agents wanted the big fish in the net, and Barnes was therefore encouraged to string Torres along and pretend to co-operate, until solid evidence could be gained against the mob. Unluckily, two factors stood in their way. The first was the criminal incompetence of John Torres. Three times the Cuban brought samples of his synthetic drugs to Philadelphia, monitored by the wiretapped Barnes. Three times it turned out that his chemist had produced the wrong formula. "The Italians", said Barnes dryly, "didn't like it."

The second factor was the Drug Enforcement Agency, which was becoming increasingly impatient with the diversion of their star witness. They needed him to testify in the Jacksonville trial of Carlos Lehder on January 12, and as the date grew nearer, the DEA pressure on the FBI to get their case concluded increased. Once Barnes had appeared in the witness box he would be thoroughly exposed, and his usefulness as an under-cover agent ended. The FBI was running out of time.

"We must have taped John Torres on a hundred different phone calls, met him 30 different times in different cities, but the FBI couldn't put the deal together," said Barnes. The DEA was livid, and to this day they still are. They say, you give the FBI anything, and they're going to screw it up."

Realising that their major objective was probably out of reach, the FBI decided to settle for what they could get. Barnes was instructed to persuade Torres to sell him some cocaine. To make the request more believable, since the Cuban knew full well that Barnes had no money and did not distribute drugs, he was to invent a brother-in-law with the right connections. This would also make an arrest easier, since the "brother-in-law" in question was a DEA agent named Sandy Tilley. Phil Akens of the FBI had wanted the role, but Barnes, artfully exploiting the principle of divide and rule, insisted that he would not fit the part.

Torres had actually met Tilley some time before, when the latter was on surveillance duty at Miami airport. Barnes, who is not without a sense of humour, had performed the introduction on his own initiative.

"I just grabbed Sandy and said, 'Hey, John, meet my brother-in-law.' It wasn't their game plan, it was mine. Sandy Tilley froze. He had a radio in his hand and had to stick it in his jacket. John Torres was so nonchalant, he didn't even recognize it."

"The FBI was mad that I got Sandy on board as my brother-in-law. It was quick thinking on his part, but John bought it just like that. Hook, line and sinker, John was hooked. He could have taken them to the heart of the Miami drug business, but they fucked it up. Not the DEA - the FBI."

Barnes and Tilley met Torres at the Mark Adams hotel in Philadelphia, where the Cuban showed them three kilograms of cocaine as an earnest of intent. He promised to supply a further 100 kilograms, to be collected in Miami. For this, the DEA man would need to produce $1,700,000 in cash. Tilley agreed to the deal.

It was just before Christmas, 1987. The smuggler and the federal agent traveled together to Florida, where they confidently expected to make a major drug bust. Everything was arranged. Well, everything except one small detail: the money.

Unlike the FBI, which has instant access to major sums for such purposes, the DEA has to manage as best it can. In this case it should not have mattered. Though miffed at the DEA involvement in the Torres affair, the Bureau still had formal responsibility, and had in fact agreed to fund the deal. Until, that is, someone remembered that the Federal Reserve Bank was closed that day.

It was a frustrating situation. Torres may not have been the brightest of God's creatures, but he had sufficient street smarts not to produce the cocaine until he saw the colour of their money.

The plan was unraveling fast. In desperation, DEA agents went to the South East Bank of Florida, which agreed to loan them the cash on one condition: it would have to be kept in a safe deposit box inside the bank. They must bring Torres to the bank, and show it to him there.

Barnes recalled: "Sandy said 'well, if this is all we have to work with, let's go to work with it. Let's see what happens.' We go to John Torres and say: 'we've got your $1.7 million, and you can come and get it $350,000 at a time, but you're going to have to come and get it out of the bank safety deposit box.'

"John Torres said: 'We just saw that last week on Miami Vice. You must be the FBI, because that's the way they do it.' Everybody laughs.

"I said: 'Come on, Sandy, you can go and get your fucking money out of the bank.' He said: 'No I can't, Andy' - kicking me. 'Not until Monday.'

"So John Torres said: 'You all do what you want. I can show you a thousand keys tonight. You can pick out a hundred.'"

A thousand kilograms. One ton of cocaine. Now they were in the major leagues. If Torres and his associates could be arrested in possession of that amount, the justice system was going to lock the door and throw away the key. Apart from anything else, that was going to make Andrew Barnes, informer, feel a lot safer. Cuban mobsters have an unpleasant reputation for wholesale revenge. But the "flash money" was in the safe deposit box, and the safe deposit box was in the bank, and there was no way that John Torres was going to step inside the doors. Barnes and Tilley cursed the imagination of the Miami Vice scriptwriters.

They did what they could, pretending that another man had been sent to fetch the money. In the meantime Torres, unaware that their meeting in Miami's Holiday Inn was being recorded by a hidden video camera, and blissfully ignorant of Tilley's identity, talked freely.

"He's saying that he's going to stitch two guys within two days," Barnes recalled, laughing. "That he's going to put his trade mark on them: two bullet holes in the head. This is all on camera, that he was going to kill them. It really helps him."

The meeting adjourned to Torres' home, where the money was supposed to be delivered. It was a family affair, with his mother bringing out three kilograms of cocaine, and his father and brother a kilogram each to show Sandy Tilley.

Then, said Barnes, "the FBI just came charging through every window in the house with machine pistols, and arrested everybody, including me and Sandy. They arrested eight people."

But the thousand kilograms of cocaine, half of which had arrived from Colombia that day, was somewhere else. By now, presumably, it is up America's nose. And all because the Federal Reserve Bank took a day off.

CHAPTER SIXTEEN
Promises, Promises

While all this was going on, the trial of Carlos Lehder and Jack Carlton-Reed was proceeding slowly, very slowly, in the U.S. District Court in Jacksonville, Florida. With ninety-five witnesses already lined up for the prosecution, Andrew Barnes was fairly confident that he would not be called to give evidence, and that was fine with him. He had a real concern that Carlos and his associates in the Medellin Cartel might take revenge on him and on his family. Besides, he reasoned, his activities on Norman's Cay were so far in the past that they were probably irrelevant to the trial.

His main concern, naturally enough, was to get the best plea bargain in his own case that he could achieve. There was little problem about this at the Miami end of the operation, as far as his post-Lehder smuggling was concerned. The FBI were so eager to retain his services in pursuit of Torres and the Philadelphia mob that he was able to get a grant of immunity with no difficulty. But in Jacksonville, U.S. Attorney Robert (Mad Dog) Merkle - so called because of his past incarnation as a Notre Dame footballer, rather then his courtroom demeanour - was proving a tougher proposition.

Merkle had had to subpoena Andrew Barnes to come to Jacksonville at all. Through the evidence of

Blankenship he was confident he had a case that would send the Englishman down for a long stretch, irrespective of whether he talked or not. The best plea-bargain offer he could make, he said, was 15 years imprisonment.

Barnes thought about it. At this point he had no lawyer, and had agreed to be de-briefed in a closed-court proceeding. "Is that straight time?" he asked.

"No," he claims he was told. "Under the federal system, if you are sentenced to 15 years you only serve five."

To Andrew Barnes that sounded very fair, and he said so. He was resigned to the fact that he would have to serve some time in prison, and five years sounded bearable. But he refused to sign anything at this point. Instead, he wisely changed his mind and asked the court to appoint him an attorney. The lawyer chosen was Russell Healey.

It was just as well. Under the sentencing guidelines operating in Florida, Healey told him, there was no hope of getting two-thirds of his sentence remitted for good behaviour.

The guidelines were strict: they took into account the volume of drugs involved in the case, and Andrew Barnes had already admitted to smuggling three tons of cocaine. Under the most generous interpretation, this meant that he would serve about nine years. He would be no better off with such a plea bargain than if he pleaded not guilty, went to trial, and lost.

But Robert Merkle was adamant. "Hell, no", he said. "That's the best deal I can make. Take it or leave it."

Barnes was in a quandary. He had a possible defense under the statute of limitations, but in view of the continuing nature of the conspiracy on Norman's Cay the government was likely to prosecute him under the RICO statute covering organised crime. In that event, his lawyer told him, he wouldn't have a leg to stand on. And the sentence might be 35 years. The prospect was not appealing. In desperation, Barnes decided to try something else. He agreed to a meeting in his attorney's office with the lawyers representing Carlos Lehder - Edward R. Shohat and Jose Quinon - after hearing from Russell Healey that they wanted to talk to him.

Robert Merkle, meanwhile, had problems of his own. The prosecution case against Lehder was not going as well as he had hoped, and though his witnesses were great in number, their quality left much to be desired. He decided he needed the testimony of Andrew Barnes. The Englishman was articulate and spoke, if he could be persuaded to speak in court, with disarming frankness. And though his involvement with Lehder was arguably stale from a legal standpoint, his evidence contained one vital factor. It would prove that Carlos Lehder, in person, had entered the United States with a load of cocaine on that first flight.

Merkle wanted to put Barnes away, but he wanted Lehder's conviction with a greater passion. All else aside, it would do him no harm when he made his run for a seat in the U.S. Senate later in the year. Privately, therefore, he was veering towards some accommodation on the issue of a plea bargain with Barnes.

But the U.S. Attorney faced another obstacle in his bid to get the pilot into the witness box. The FBI was very unwilling to allow it, for once their star informant stood up in public, his usefulness as an undercover agent against John Torres and Co would be at an end. And their investigation of the case was going much more slowly than had been hoped. Angrily, Robert Merkle gave the FBI an ultimatum: finish your business with Barnes within a month, or I will subpoena him anyway.

Andrew Barnes had more going for him than he knew, when he met with Shohat and Quinon in Russell Healey's office on February 8, 1988. Also present were Stephen J. Weinbaum, attorney for Jack Carlton Reed, and a private detective employed by Lehder's defence. It was an extraordinary meeting, later to become the subject of a fierce wrangle in the courtroom. Barnes was making a bid to have a personal interview with Carlos Lehder, incarcerated under massive security on the top floor of the Jacksonville Post Office building. The question was, why ? Why should he have been so anxious to talk to the Colombian, whom he had not seen for more than six years?   Robert Merkle was to make valiant efforts to find out. He never did.

The meeting with Lehder's attorneys did not go well though Barnes, by his own account, was at first assured that Carlos held him in high regard and wanted to see him. He began by recounting the story of his first trip to Colombia, but once he had told them he would not be testifying at the trial they stopped him in mid-flow. They would not permit him to see their client, to speak with him on the telephone, or to write letters to him. They wanted Andrew Barnes to have no contact with Carlos Lehder.

The reason for their attitude was fairly obvious. If a meeting between the two became known to the prosecution, as it undoubtedly would, Lehder's defence against a conspiracy charge would be demonstrably weakened. The Colombian's lawyers may already have been nervous, for their luncheon meeting with Russell Healey the previous day, at which the meeting with Barnes had been set up, had been observed by chief DEA agent Douglas Driver.

In any case, if, as Barnes was claiming at this point, he had no intention of giving evidence against their client, the Englishman was totally irrelevant. Of course, they said, if he changed his mind about appearing in court, they would be interested to have advance notice of what he intended to say.

Andrew Barnes did not give up that easily. He had brought to the meeting a letter and a card of condolence, both of which he asked Shohat and Quinon to pass on to Lehder. They agreed to do so, at least verbally. They also agreed to keep the contents confidential. In this, they lied.

Bearing in mind the circumstances, and the character of both writer and recipient, the message on the card that Barnes gave to the lawyers that day was fairly remarkable. It began with a printed salutation: *"To Carlos. May the sincere concern of those who care help you through this difficult time."* Below this Barnes had written: *"I was with you in the beginning and will not abandon you at the end. Don't give up, Carlos. We will beat this thing together, and some day we will fly again with the eagles. You are greatly admired and loved. God Bless You. Love, Andy."*

"Basically," Barnes was later to explain in court, "the card is one to encourage Carlos not to give up spiritually and anything else like that."

Spirituality is not the first quality that springs to mind when discussing Carlos Lehder. Nor Andrew Barnes either, for that matter. Which makes the remainder of the writing on the card all the more bizarre. Barnes had written:

"The lord is my shepherd. I shall not want. He maketh me to lie down in green pastures. He leadeth me beside the still waters. He restoreth my soul. He leadeth me in

the path of righteousness for his name's sake. Yea, though I walk in the valley of the shadow of death I will fear no evil. For thou art with me. Thy rod and thy staff they comfort me. Thou preparest a table before me in the presence of mine enemies. Thou anointest my head with oil. My cup runneth over. Surely, goodness and mercy shall follow me all the days of my life, and I will dwell in the house of the Lord forever."

Psalm 23. Anything less applicable to the circumstances would be hard to imagine. "The card conveys my sentiments towards him about keeping the faith in God," Barnes was to tell the court later.

Perhaps it was some form of code. The accompanying letter was certainly full of nuance, once one knows what Andrew Barnes was actually trying to say. It read:

"Dear Carlos,

I am happy to be able to communicate with you again, but of course I wish it were under different circumstances. I am here in Jacksonville under Federal subpoena*. They are going to charge me with one count of conspiracy to import, and one count of conspiracy to violate RICO. I could get 35 years if convicted.

"Since I am basically indigent, I have been appointed a court-appointed lawyer. His name is Russell Healey. He is very sharp and I am pleased with his efforts for me. We plea-bargained with U.S. Attorney Merkle and

the Assistant U.S. Attorney, Mueller, for a seven year cap on my sentence, but negotiations broke down.

"After I told Merkle that the part of the deal I couldn't live with was testifying against you, he got more irritated or mad when I told him you were the finest man I have met, and stormed out of the room. So here I am. I intend to fight the battle to the end.

"Healey says I have two choices for a defense. The first is arguing that the statute of limitations has expired. The government contends that this is invalid, as you allegedly continued the conspiracy even without me. The second defense is just to let them try me. The only witness so far against me is that moron, idiot, traitor, you-name-it, Blankenship.

"I do not know where Greenberger or Bush are, or where they stand concerning me or you. My wife Barbara knows that I can win this, and I want you to know I have her full support in doing anything I can to help you, even it gets me into more trouble.

"That is how much effect you have had on our lives, even though our liaison was very brief. You knew me as a young boy, very unreliable and full of partying etc. I wish we had met a little later in life. I have matured considerably since then. But I still truly treasure some of our memories.

"I finally mastered the C.46 and went on to captain one for five years, and 3,000 hours of flight from Africa

*to South America. I am sorry I embarrassed you
with that last boo-boo.*

*"We now have three children. Andy Jr. is twelve
years old and remembers you well. And we have two
girls, Amanda and Katey. Barbara sells real estate up
in Pennsylvania and is happy there as her whole family
lives within twenty miles of us.*

*"I have done just about everything that can be done.
I have driven tractor-trailer trucks, crewed sailboats,
delivered bread. You name it, I've tried it. I was
arrested in North Eluthera two years ago and served
some time in Foxhill Prison in Nassau. I finally got
Arlington Butler to convince the magistrate that I had no
money and let me and my co-pilot go.*

*"I was arrested at Paitilla airport in Panama and
they confiscated my twin Beech E-18 about a year ago.
I think Merkle is trying to make a big deal out of this
business because of all the Noriega nonsense he is
stirring up. But it is all bull-crap, all the Noriega
stuff.*

*"Anyway, Joe, it would take a year of talk for us to
catch up on all that has happened, so I won't try now. I
do hope if we have to do some time on this thing that
Jack, you and me can be together somewhere.*

*"Anyway, let's not think anything negative yet. But
you have my promise, and I will be riding down the path
you make. I will not waver. I have seen and done
enough things in this crazy world that I know what I*

mean when I commit myself to a certain course of action. I will stand by you Joe, no matter what. I have asked my attorney, Russell Healey, to contact your attorney, Ed Shohat, and convey my sentiments to you. I have even asked your lawyer if I can see you for a short time. I will not get an answer to any of these questions until tomorrow.

"I have bought some Fleetwood Mack and Stevie Nix tapes for you. I remember how much you like this group. Me too. Anyway, if your lawyer says no I will give him this letter and the tapes.

"Please put Barbara on your visiting list as she wants to see you too. I understand there may be a conflict with your attorney on this arrangement, but at this point I don't believe that it makes any difference.

"I hope to be able to see you, Joe. If for some reason I can't, please write the address I gave you and contact Russell Healey. Card is enclosed. Of course, I don't know what is going to happen to me yet. They may just arrest me as our plea agreement went bust, or I will be free until the end of your trial and then be indicted and arrested. I am not scared. We have to stay together, Joe. Love, Andy."

*"So far I am under my own recognisant bond, but that could change quickly. I refuse to co-operate."

265

From a man who was already co-operating with everyone in sight in an effort to save his neck, the last sentence was a touch far-fetched. Particularly in view of the fact that Barnes had already received a subpoena to testify in the Lehder trial, dated January 10. No matter, Lehder was not to know that.

There is some doubt that the Colombian even read the letter, but he certainly read a second one, written the following day, on February 9. Andrew Barnes, apparently distrusting Messrs. Shohat and Quinon, sent Lehder another missive - this time through the U.S. mail. This one, he knew, would be read by the U.S. Marshals who were guarding the prisoner. He couched it accordingly:

"Dear Carlos,

I have missed you greatly, and I am very happy to be able to write to you. Obviously I wish the circumstances were different. I have made several attempts to communicate with you while I am down in Jacksonville, but have been frustrated by your sea of lawyers, who seem convinced that I may mitigate (sic) your situation by doing so. Anyway, I know that Shohat and Jose are only looking out for your best interests, and I am impressed with their grasp of this case. "I gave Shohat a card from Barbara and myself, and he did say he would relay the contents of this to you verbally. I hope he keeps his word. I will keep this letter short for the same reasons given. I am writing this because I don't expect him to deliver the other letter.

"Don't give up, Joe. You are much admired and loved by us all. It seems that you have fallen victim to a very large machine that is about to take me down with it too. I will be indicted on the so-called second wave of indictments. I am not scared or worried. Why worry when there is nothing you can do about it? I hope Shohat explains my position to you. I will not hurt you. I refuse to testify against you - not that I could say anything anyway.

"Barbara and myself live in Pennsylvania now, out in the country where it is quiet and pretty. We have three children: one boy and two girls. Barbara has bought you a tape collection of old and new Fleetwood Mack tapes. We would like to see you as soon as it is feasible. Barbara sells real estate now. Her whole family lives within 20 miles of our house, so no matter what happens to me she has some support.

"The court appointed me a lawyer, Russell Healey. He is very sharp and I am pleased with his efforts for me. He says I have a real good shot at beating this.

"Remember, please call. I will do anything I can for you. Let's maintain our friendship. We will beat this rap together. I am not going anywhere, Carlos. I will be there, always be there. God bless you.

Love, Andy."

There cannot have been a dry eye in the cell after this outpouring of affection. However, what was it all about? Robert Merkle was to do his best to find out, but at the time he knew nothing of the existence of the letters, and was not to learn of them until Barnes was under cross-examination in the Lehder trial six weeks later. He did know, however, of the meeting with Lehder's lawyers, having been tipped off by Douglas Driver. It concentrated his mind wonderfully.

Suddenly, it had become a matter of urgency to strike a deal with Barnes before the opposition got to him and possibly persuaded the Englishman not to testify. His previously adamant insistence on a 15-year sentence vanished, and Russell Healey was able to negotiate a plea bargain deal on Barnes' behalf which guaranteed a maximum sentence of seven years imprisonment, plus a possible fine of up to $25,000.

The bargain was actually signed on March 4, 1988, though its major provisions had been agreed on February 17. Under its terms, Barnes was to plead guilty to one count of conspiracy to import cocaine. He would not be charged with any other offence. In return, he would agree to testify fully and truthfully at the trial of Carlos Lehder, and any subsequent trials that might arise.

With that offer on the table, the earnest pledges made to Carlos Lehder nine days before vanished from Andrew Barnes' mind like morning mist. He reckoned he had a good deal. He signed on the dotted line.

CHAPTER SEVENTEEN
Choosing Sides

That plea bargain agreement became the subject of instant controversy when the cross-examination of Andrew Barnes in the Lehder trial began on March 28, 1988. Jose Quinon denounced it as "a sham". He told Robert Merkle, in a side-bar encounter with the judge: "I am taking the position that you drafted a plea agreement that nobody can understand for the purpose of hiding this man's deal....I am entitled to show this jury that there are tools available to this prosecutor that he has chosen not to exercise because this individual is a witness in this case." It got him nowhere. As Merkle pointed out mildly, the court had had no problem in understanding the agreement.

Quinon's rage was understandable. Barnes' testimony had been extremely damaging to his client, and given the Englishman's attitude at their meeting on February 8 it smacked distinctly of betrayal. There was another factor involved, too. But he would not, could not, speak of that. To do so might blow the defense case out of the water. Whatever else happened, Andrew Barnes must not be asked the question that would expose everything that had been implied during that meeting.

And so Jose Quinon concentrated on the plea bargain agreement, seeking to prove that Barnes had been coerced into giving evidence by threats against his wife.

"During the course of your testimony here," he asked, "did the government tell you they had listed your wife as a co-conspirator in this case?"

Andrew Barnes: *No, they did not.*

Mr Quinon: *All right, you testified that your wife brought a car to you one time, and she knew at that time that the car was going to be used for the transportation of cocaine. Is that correct?*

Andrew Barnes: *Correct.*

Mr Quinon: *And she knew you were involved in the cocaine business?*

Andrew Barnes: *Correct.*

Mr Quinon: *And she was benefiting from whatever profits you were deriving from the cocaine business?*

Andrew Barnes: *Correct.*

Mr Quinon: *Furthermore, you have also testified that she had given some keys to Rocky, so that he could move a car that supposedly had around 300 kilos of cocaine in it. Is that correct?*

Andrew Barnes: *Correct.*

Mr Quinon: *And you knew then that she knew what was contained in the car?*

Andrew Barnes: *Yes, she was aware of what was in the car.*

Mr Quinon: *Because you had told her that?*

Andrew Barnes: *Yes.*

Mr Quinon: *And knowing the contents of the car, did the government tell you that was sufficient to charge her as a conspirator in this case, as much as you were? That she was as guilty as you were.*

Andrew Barnes: *No, the words I can remember were that the government's position was that they were only interested in prosecuting major figures in this, and sideline figures such as my wife would not be prosecuted.*

Mr Quinon: *When did the government tell you that?*

Andrew Barnes: *I can't recall, but it had to do with that conversation about my wife. It was a concern of mine.*

Jose Quinon scented blood. *"You had concern that your wife would be charged. You didn't want that to happen. Correct?"* he pressed.

Andrew Barnes: *That's exactly right.*

Mr Quinon: *And the reason for that is that you have three children?*

Andrew Barnes: *Correct.*

Mr Quinon: *If you had to do whatever time you have to do, you wouldn't want your wife put away as well, because then nobody could watch the children. Correct?*

Andrew Barnes: *That's correct. I was going to take the heat.*

Mr Quinon: *And so, when that came out at the first meeting, they said: 'Don't worry about it; we're not going to charge her because she's a peripheral character in all this?'*

Andrew Barnes: *I don't recall which meeting it was, but it was brought up.*

Mr Quinon: *Or did they tell you that if you didn't plead, not only would they indict you, but they would indict her?*

Andrew Barnes: *No sir, that didn't occur that way.*

Mr Quinon: *Were you concerned that they would indict her if you didn't plead in this case?*

Andrew Barnes: *No. I was sufficiently convinced that she played such a minor role, directly at my insistence, that I couldn't believe that they would make a case against her.*

Jose Quinon raised his eyebrows. *"You couldn't believe that?"*

Andrew Barnes: *Yes, I was even offered a letter to that effect.*

Mr Quinon: *You were even offered a letter?*

Andrew Barnes: *Yes, but I said that would not be necessary.*

Mr Quinon: *Who offered you that letter?*

Andrew Barnes: *I believe, Ernst Mueller.*

Mr Quinon: *When did he tell you that?*

Andrew Barnes: *He was outlining a scenario that didn't exist. The way I read it was that my wife was not being dangled in front of me in order to make my decision.*

Jose Quinon was getting nowhere. He switched tack, suggesting that Barnes had caved in to federal pressure under threat of a massive jail sentence, and was prepared to lie under oath to get it reduced. He still got nowhere. Barnes remained firm that he was testifying of his own free will. He also resisted any suggestion that his request for a meeting with Quinon's client was motivated by a desire to get incriminating evidence on the Colombian, which he could then pass to the authorities. And though the subsequent questioning on the involvement of his son, and an embarrassed reading of the text of the letters sent to Lehder, did little to gain him sympathy with the jury, his evidence remained intact.

Andrew Barnes had been a model witness for the prosecution. His performance might have been expected to win him a few brownie points with Robert Merkle. It did not. The reason was that until they were produced in court, the U.S. Attorney had not seen the letters; had had no inkling of their existence. Now he was faced with the fact that the amiable Englishman had been playing footsie with the opposition, or at least trying to do so. And what did that mean in terms of his evidence? Whose side was Barnes on? Robert Merkle was fit to be tied. Angrily, he told the judge at side-bar that he intended to re-examine the witness, to treat him as hostile, and to impeach him.

It was not easy. Merkle's questioning was subjected to a constant barrage of objections by the opposing attorneys who seemed, in an odd reversal of roles, to have adopted Andrew Barnes as a client. Or perhaps they were merely concerned that the motives behind the meeting on February 8 should not be too deeply probed.

It seemed fairly safe, however, to ask Barnes why he had chosen to quote the 23rd Palm.

"It's my favourite psalm," came the bland reply. "It's something to comfort one in trouble."

Mr Merkle: *It's a supplication to God for righteousness? Did you write: "He leadeth me in the paths of righteousness" - isn't that part of the psalm?*

Andrew Barnes: *That's correct*

Mr. Merkle: *Later, in another letter, you told Mr. Lehder that you would follow him in any path he chooses. Do you recall that?*

Andrew Barnes: *That's correct.*

Mr. Merkle: *Do you mean to suggest in that letter to Mr. Lehder that you and he had been marching down the path of ....*

"Objection!" cried Jose Quinon.

Judge: *Let him answer the question as to what he meant.*
Andrew Barnes: *I was trying to tell Carlos that there was another way we could go; that we could get out of this mess and carry on.*

Mr Merkle: *What way is that?*

Andrew Barnes: *Well, the way I'm doing it is to make amends for what I have done by pleading guilty.*

Jose Quinon: *Objection! Objection!!* (was this guy suggesting that Carlos Lehder should have done the same thing?)

Not for the first time, nor the last, both attorneys were summoned to the side bench.

"I request the court's patience to allow me to develop this line of questioning," said Robert Merkle. "I've worked extensively on it. It's appropriate and necessary. We've put this whole issue in front of the jury in those letters. He's lied on this witness stand as to why, and I know he lied.   I'm going to bring it out in my cross-examination.

"But if every time I ask a leading question it's interrupted, and you sustain the objection, I can't do it. The rule provides that I can impeach this man, and the only way I can get......"

Even Mad Dog Merkle could not get away with talking to a judge like that.

"Just a minute," retorted Judge Howell W. Melton, a silver-haired man of   cherubic features and normally mild demeanour.   "Don't tell me what I can do and what I can't do.   If he shows he is hostile...."

Robert Merkle interrupted.   "He is hostile," he insisted.   "Your honour, I can't sit here and tell you all the information I have.   The point is you don't have enough information before you to judge whether the leading question is necessary or not."

The learned conversation drifted off into an argument as to whether Andrew Barnes could be asked what Psalm 23 meant to the people of Israel.   This issue seemed some way from the smuggling of cocaine, and the judge confessed that he certainly didn't know the answer.   "He may know," he said wearily, "and you can develop that. If you have information that he does know, fine.   But I don't think you can say that."

But Robert Merkle was not about to give up, even on such an arcane point.   "That's interesting," he retorted, "because you allowed defense attorneys to ask him leading questions on his understanding of the law, when he clearly has no understanding of the law. I think the same rules apply to the government when they are impeaching a witness. I'm allowed to ask leading questions. I don't have to show first that he understands."

It was possibly not a good way to win friends and influence judges.

Replied Judge Melton: "I will say this: I have been about as patient as any man could possibly be. With the whole group of you. Sometimes it wears thin, but I've tried to be patient, I'm going to be patient...... I will be patient," - he was going to be patient or die in the attempt - "but you must also be patient and understanding when the court rules. That's not because I don't like you, or that I don't like Mr. Quinon......"

Mr Merkle: *Oh, I didn't suggest that.* (Perish the thought!)

Judge Melton: *I know that. I know that. I know that. I know that. I'm just trying to bring it down to basics. I'm just trying to do the best I can here. If it doesn't satisfy you, I'm sorry. I'm just going to rule on it...*

Mr Merkle (interrupting): *I just want the court to understand there's an entire line of questioning in which there will have to be leading questions about these letters.*

Now, if he (Mr. Quinon) *is going to stand up and yell at you every time I ask a leading question it's going to make it very difficult. I understand you have to rule on each and every question that appears improper. My understanding at this point is that this witness has clearly demonstrated that he's a hostile witness. He has clearly withheld information. I am telling the court that there are matters not covered by Mr. Quinon that have got to be covered, and can only be covered in a leading fashion.*

"Oh, all right,' said Judge Melton finally. "But you'll have to ask the non-leading questions first." Truly a judgment of Solomon. Andrew Barnes braced his shoulders and prepared once more for combat.

Mr Merkle: *The letter says: 'I was with you in the beginning' What were you referring to at that point?*

Andrew Barnes: *The beginning of the Norman's Cay operation.*

Mr Merkle: *And you say: 'Don't give up, Carlos, we will beat this thing together.' What were you proposing to him?*

Andrew Barnes: *I was proposing to him not so much to beat the law on this thing, but to beat this problem we*

have. The problem of being outlaws, or renegades,
or sinners

Mr Merkle: *Are you saying you weren't telling Mr.*
Lehder that you proposed that you would beat the
charges in this case together?

Andrew Barnes: *No, I wasn't referring to that.*

Mr Merkle: *When you say "beat this thing", what were*
you referring to?

Andrew Barnes: *By that I mean this ugliness, this evil. I*
found great comfort in reading such psalms as this in my
short and troubled life.

Mr Merkle: *That sentence continues: "some day we'll*
fly again where only eagles dare."

Andrew Barnes: *That's correct.*

Mr. Merkle: *Did you mean by that to propose that you*
fly drugs again?

Jose Quinon was on his feet in flash. His objection
was overruled.

Andrew Barnes: *It wasn't to mean drugs necessarily. No, certainly not.*

Mr Merkle: *Where is that you've flown with Mr. Lehder 'where only eagles dare?'*

Andrew Barnes: *I only flew with Carlos one time, and that was on the drug smuggling trip to Colombia.*

Mr Merkle: *That's not true, is it.*

Andrew Barnes: *Well, I have flown with him on other trips.*

Mr Merkle: *How many times?*

Andrew Barnes: *Only once to Colombia.*

Mr Merkle: *Was that a place where only eagles dare to fly?*

Andrew Barnes: *It could be. I suppose I meant that.*

Mr Merkle: *Why do you use that particular term, 'where only eagles dare?' What's your understanding of that term?*

Andrew Barnes: *It's tricky. It's like the ultimate - the hardest place to fly.*

Mr Merkle: *The most dangerous?*

Andrew Barnes: *The most dangerous.*

Mr Merkle: *Now, there's nothing dangerous about flying to Colombia, just to fly to Colombia?*

Andrew Barnes: *No.*

Mr Merkle: *And you testified you flew to Pine Cay. Is that correct?*

Andrew Barnes: *Correct.*

Mr Merkle: *Is there anything dangerous about flying to Pine Cay?*

Andrew Barnes: *No.*

Mr Merkle: *And on one occasion to Lubbock, etc. Anything dangerous about your making these flights?*

Andrew Barnes: *No.*

Mr Merkle: *What is it about your trips with Mr. Lehder that makes them dangerous, in the sense that only eagles would dare fly?*

Andrew Barnes: *It's dangerous when you are loaded with cocaine.*

Now that was what Robert Merkle wanted to hear. He pressed his advantage.

Mr Merkle: *My question to you is this: were you proposing to Mr. Lehder, or suggesting to him, or wanting him to believe that you hoped to fly drugs with him again?*

Andrew Barnes: *I was trying to...the whole spirit of the thing was to give him hope that one day he'll be out of this mess, just like me, and we can carry on.*

Mr Merkle: *Carry on doing what?*

Andrew Barnes: *Well, I didn't necessarily mean hauling drugs.*

Robert Merkle had made his point.

"Well, Mr. Barnes," he continued. "Take a look at that letter you wrote that same day. You testified on cross-examination concerning a particular phrase on the front page. First of all, you say: 'I'm so happy to be able to communicate with you again.' Is that a true statement?"

Andrew Barnes: *Yes.*

Mr Merkle: *I believe you signed that letter `Love, Andy'. Correct?*

Andrew Barnes: *That's how I sign all my letters.*
Mr Merkle: *To everybody?*

Andrew Barnes: *No, not to everybody.*

Mr Merkle: *You wouldn't sign a letter to me "Love, Andy" would you?*

It seemed increasingly unlikely.

Andrew Barnes: *No. Somebody I cared about.*

Mr Merkle: *In your second letter, on February 9, you signed it: `God Bless you, Love Andy'. Correct?*

Andrew Barnes: *Yes.*

Mr Merkle: *Why were you so happy to communicate with him again?*

Andrew Barnes: *Well, I hadn't seen or heard from Carlos in a long time, and of course I said I wished it were under different circumstances.*

Mr Merkle: *Look at the letter of February 9. You start out in much the same way.*

Andrew Barnes: *I assumed the first letter wasn't going to be delivered.*

Mr Merkle: *You say: `My dear Carlos, I have missed you greatly....'   Now, when did you start missing Mr. Lehder, Mr. Barnes?   You testified that you left Norman's Cay in December 1980. Did you start missing him then?*

Andrew Barnes: *Yes, sir. I mean, I hadn't seen him since the end of 1980 until today.*

Mr Merkle: *Did you miss him greatly in 1981?*

Andrew Barnes: *I have missed Carlos, not seeing him, since I hadn't last seen him, if that's what you mean.*

Mr Merkle: *No, my question is: did you miss him greatly in 1981.*

Andrew Barnes: *No, not particularly.*

Mr Merkle: *1982?*

Andrew Barnes: *No sir, not particularly. Like I said....*
Mr Merkle: *Did you miss him greatly in 1983?*

Andrew Barnes: *I missed working for Carlos because the money wasn't there, obviously.*

Mr Merkle: *Mr. Barnes, did you say in that letter: I miss working for you?*

Andrew Barnes: *Yeah, I sure have.*

Mr Merkle: *In that sentence, is that what you said?*

Andrew Barnes: *Yeah.*

Mr Merkle: *In that sentence, where does it say that, Mr. Barnes? Does it say "I miss working for you"?*

Andrew Barnes: *No, it doesn't.*

Mr Merkle: *All right. In 1984 did you miss Mr. Lehder greatly?*

Andrew Barnes: *No, sir.*

Mr Merkle: *1985?*

Andrew Barnes: *Not particularly.*

Mr Merkle: *1986?*

Andrew Barnes: *No. I mean I....* (he could see where they were heading)

Mr Merkle: *You didn't miss him at all, did you Mr. Barnes? In fact, on the day you wrote this letter you didn't miss him. Isn't that true?*

Andrew Barnes: *Well, it all...like I said...I'm not attaching too much great significance to this letter.*

But Robert Merkle was. The "mad dog" had his teeth locked fast. He would not let it go.

Mr Merkle: *Well, we will try and find out what you attached to it at the time. It's not a true statement, is it?*
Andrew Barnes: *Literally, if you were to use the word "miss" like that - like you would miss your kids, or miss your home town - no.*

Mr. Merkle: *Let me ask you this, Mr. Barnes. You said "I am very happy to be able to write you." Assuming you missed Mr. Lehder greatly. You testified in cross-examination that you followed very closely the events surrounding Mr. Lehder's arrest and extradition from Colombia.*

Andrew Barnes: *That's correct.*

Mr Merkle: *And that occurred in February 1987, did it not?*

Andrew Barnes: *That's correct.*

Mr Merkle: *Did you write to him then?*

Andrew Barnes: *No, I didn't.*

Mr Merkle: *Did you try to?*

Andrew Barnes: *No, I didn't.*

Mr Merkle: *When you read about the trial, back in November, did you write to him then?*

Andrew Barnes: *No, I didn't.*

Mr Merkle: *Did you try to?*

Andrew Barnes: *No.*

Mr Merkle: *Did you miss him at all?*

Andrew Barnes: *No.*

Mr Merkle: *In fact, is it not true that what you told this jury on cross-examination, that this was a letter of love and support, is a total falsehood?*

Andrew Barnes: *It could be construed that way, yes.*
Mr Merkle: *Please answer the question, Mr. Barnes.*
Andrew Barnes: *Yes, it was.*

Point made.

Mr Merkle: *Let's continue with that first letter. You say on the second page: `the second defence is to just let them try me. The only witness so far against me is that moron, idiot, traitor, you name it - Blankenship.' Did you write that?*

Andrew Barnes: *Yes, I did.*

Mr Merkle: *Did you call Mr. Blankenship a liar in that sentence?*

Andrew Barnes: *No, I didn't*

Mr. Merkle: *Why did you call him a traitor?*

Andrew Barnes: *Because I felt like he betrayed me for...*

Mr Merkle: *For doing what? For lying about you, or telling the truth about you?*

Andrew Barnes: *No, he didn't lie about me. He told the truth.*

Mr Merkle: *Then you say: `I do not know where Greenberger or Bush are, or where they stand concerning me or you..' What's the purpose in communicating that to Mr. Lehder?*

Andrew Barnes: *I was trying to find out if he knew where they stood in relevance to us.*

Mr Merkle: *What do you mean by that? Whether they are going to co-operate and testify against you and Mr. Lehder?*

Andrew Barnes: *That's correct.*

Mr Merkle: *Did you discuss that with Mr. Lehder's defence attorneys when you met them?*

Andrew Barnes: *I believe so, yes.*

Mr Merkle: *What did they tell you?*

Andrew Barnes: *They had no word on Greenberger or Bush.*

Mr Merkle: *Mr. Quinon asked you if were true that they led you to believe that the letters would not become public. Is that correct?*

Andrew Barnes: *That's correct.*

Mr Merkle: *Did Mr. Quinon at any time tell you why the letters became public?*

Andrew Barnes: *No, he never did.*

Mr Merkle: *Did you rely on whatever assurances Mr. Quinon gave you?*

Andrew Barnes: *Yes, I did.*

Mr Merkle: *Was there a specific reason why it was discussed that the letters should be hand-delivered or orally reported to Mr. Lehder, as opposed to being sent through the mail?*

Andrew Barnes: (Pausing) *The U.S. mail is subject, in Lehder's case, to being read.*

Mr Merkle: *Who brought that to your attention?*

Andrew Barnes: *Ed Shohat did.*

Mr Merkle: *What if any concern did he express about that?*

Andrew Barnes: *He said that sending it through the post was not the right way to do it. It was monitored......I was just told that they had a hard time getting mail to him through the Marshal's service, and they would orally convey what I had written.*

Mr Merkle: *Did they tell you that in fact the U.S. government does not get that information?*

Andrew Barnes: *No, they didn't.*

Mr Merkle: *You never advised the U.S. government that you wrote these letters to Mr. Lehder, did you?*

Andrew Barnes: *No, I never did.*

Mr Merkle: *You state in the letter on the first page: negotiations broke down after I told Merkle that the part of the deal I couldn't live with was testifying against you.' Was that true, Mr. Barnes?*

Andrew Barnes: *No, that's really not that true.*

Mr Merkle: *How true is it?*

Andrew Barnes: *It's not true at all.*

Mr Merkle: *Did you at any time tell me you couldn't live with testifying against Mr. Lehder?*

Andrew Barnes: *That's true.   That's utterly true. Look, the reason for these letters, and the long and short of it again, is to try and find out information for myself that I wasn't getting anywhere through other means.*

Mr Merkle: *But there was another reason, too, wasn't there?*

Andrew Barnes: *There were other reasons, yes.*

Indeed there were.   Robert Merkle was coming close to the crux of the question.   And then, inexplicably, he backed away.

"We'll come to those in a minute," he said.   *"If that is not true, about telling me that you couldn't live with testifying against Lehder, do I take it that the first sentence following that - 'He got even more irritated and mad when I told him you were the finest man I had ever met and stormed out of the room' - Is that also not true?"*

Andrew Barnes: *That's not true.*

Mr Merkle: *Turn to page 2. You say there: 'My wife, Barbara knows that I can win this, and I want you to know that I have her full support in doing anything I can do to help you, even if it gets me into more trouble.' Is that true, Mr. Barnes?*

Andrew Barnes: *No, that's not true.*

Mr. Merkle: *Did your wife know that you wrote this letter?*

Andrew Barnes: *No, she didn't*

Mr. Merkle: *Did she see it?*

Andrew Barnes: *She never saw the letter.*

Mr. Merkle: *Mr. Barnes, you testified that your wife met Mr. Lehder once in 1978, for about twenty minutes out at the airport. And when was the next time she met him?*
Andrew Barnes: *She only met him once in the '78 time-frame. The next time was when we went over to see Joe the second time.*

Mr Merkle: *You had lunch on that occasion?*

Andrew Barnes: *That's correct, we stayed over all the afternoon.*

Mr Merkle: *How many hours?*

Andrew Barnes: *Maybe three or four hours.*

Mr Merkle: *Three or four hours. And that's a year and a half after being in his presence for twenty minutes. Correct?*

Andrew Barnes: *Correct.*

Mr Merkle: *After that occasion, how many times did your wife get together with Mr. Lehder?*

Andrew Barnes: *Maybe four or five times after that.*

Mr Merkle: *Where?*

Andrew Barnes: *At Norman's Cay.*

Mr Merkle: *For what purpose?*

Andrew Barnes: *She was either riding over with me with groceries, or when we came back from Minnesota in the Cessna 310 with the Robertson STOL kit on it.*

Mr Merkle: *These were business trips?*

Andrew Barnes: *That's correct.*

Mr Merkle: *Were you and your wife socialising with Mr Lehder; going out to dinner with him?*

Andrew Barnes: *On that one occasion we had dinner with him. Everybody used to have dinner in the same house at that time.*

Mr Merkle: *Did your wife correspond with Mr. Lehder?*

Andrew Barnes: *No.*

Mr Merkle: *Did your wife miss Mr. Lehder?*

Andrew Barnes: *No.*

Mr Merkle: *Now, if its not true that your wife fully supported any effort to help Mr. Lehder, why did you say that?*

Andrew Barnes: *I felt all along on this thing that the burden has been on Carlos. Not all culpability, but the burden of people like me being here. I was drug into this thing on an indictment that brought him here, that I wasn't even involved with on Norman's Cay at the time.*

There is a little bit of feeling of backlash. The reason Carlos is up here is for things he did when I wasn't even on Norman's Cay, and I was getting in gear to fight the charges I was getting charged with. But obviously I didn't have a leg to stand on; that's why I plea-bargained.

Mr Merkle: *You just testified to feeling some hostility to Mr Lehder. Is that correct?*

Andrew Barnes: *Not hostility, but definitely he ought to understand that people like me are a little row-boat sitting next to the Titanic going down.*

Mr Merkle: *Now, Andy Jr., you testified, flew with you on your loads in 1980.*

Andrew Barnes: *That's correct.*

Mr Merkle: *Was he able to read and write at that time?*

Andrew Barnes: *I can't recall.*

Mr Merkle: *I believe you testified that on those times you got a call to come and pick up the children for school?*

Andrew Barnes: *That's correct.*

Mr Merkle: *You testified that you would taxi the aircraft to the hangar and load it with cocaine?*

Andrew Barnes: *Yes.*

Mr. Merkle: *How long would you stay on the island on each of those occasions?*

Andrew Barnes: *Approximately half an hour. We would top off the aircraft; the fuel tanks.*

Mr Merkle: *Strictly business?*

Andrew Barnes: *Strictly business.*

Mr Merkle: *And where was little Andy staying while that was going on?*

Andrew Barnes: *He'd be running around, inside or outside the hangar, playing with his cars or something.*

Mr Merkle: *You state in your letter that 'Andy Jr. remembers you well.' He doesn't, does he?*

Andrew Barnes: *He remembers going over to Norman's Cay and flying aeroplanes.*

Mr Merkle: *But does he know the difference between Joe Lehder and Adam's house cat, Mr. Barnes? Does little Andy remember Carlos Lehder well?*

Andrew Barnes: *If he were to walk in the door of this courtroom at this time, I doubt if he could pick out Carlos Lehder.*

Mr Merkle: *Has he talked to you frequently about Mr. Lehder over the past few years?*

Andrew Barnes: *No.*

Mr Merkle: *Has he expressed any missing or longing for Mr. Lehder?*

Andrew Barnes: *No.*

Mr Merkle: *Has he corresponded with Mr. Lehder?*

Andrew Barnes: *No.*

Mr Merkle: *Is that statement true or false, that he remembers Mr. Lehder well?*

Andrew Barnes: *That statement is obviously false.*

Robert Merkle switched to Barnes' experience in Panama, and his mention of it in the letter to Lehder. It was to be a diversion that would cost the court a lot of time.

"Is it not a fact," he said, "that you wanted to communicate to Mr. Lehder your support of him, and of Mr. Noriega?"

Barnes never got a chance to answer. There was a storm of protest from defence counsel, and both attorneys were called to the bench.

"I've never met anybody more unethical than this man," said Jose Quinon when they reached the judge's side. "I object to that strongly," retorted Robert Merkle. Both men were shouting, their words carrying plainly to the rest of the court.

"Keep your voice down," said Judge Melton, but he was clearly wasting his breath. He sent the jury out, lest the ensuring fight should sully their judgement. As the door closed behind them, Robert Merkle returned to his own defence.

"I want the record to reflect that counsel yelled at me, and pointed his finger in the presence of the jury," he cried. "I have never seen anybody so unethical as this man. It's outrageous."

Quinon was unimpressed. "This is Mr. Merkle," he said, "doing his usual show-boating, which he enjoys dearly, n front of the jury on this case. He has done it continuously.   He has not heeded your rulings, went ahead and yelled in front of the jury.....I will tell you this. I mean what I said, because I think this is the most unethical prosecutor I have met with in a courtroom for the 13 years I have been practising - including the four years I have been prosecuting myself."

Given more time to think, Jose Quinon might have put that differently.

Merkle retorted sarcastically: "I can see why the chief judge of the llth circuit found it necessary to tell the ABA that the American Bar Association had essentially sold out to drug money.   It is tragic to hear that kind of comment and see the defence make this kind of manipulation in this courtroom.

"The fact is that Mr. Quinon has not been accused by me of unethical conduct, nor has he been shouted at by me, or been the subject of the concerted attack mounted against the ethics of the prosecution since this trial started. This is orchestrated.   It's deliberate, it's intended, and it's having an effect."

The wrangle went on for three-quarters of an hour, ostensibly because Robert Merkle had dared to infer a link between Carlos Lehder and General Noriega, the Panamanian dictator accused of drug-running.   In the end, a desperately neutral Judge Melton had had enough. He threatened an action for contempt of court against anyone who as much as mentioned the name of Noriega again.

"Clear enough, gentlemen?" he said.   "Anybody not understand that?   No more Noriega, period."

The trial of Carlos Lehder, and the prosecution's re-examination of Andrew Barnes were resumed.   By that time, of course, most people in court had completely lost the thread.

Even before the interruption, Robert Merkle had been wandering.   He had established that the letters to Lehder were not worth the paper they were written on, but he had got no closer to finding out what Barnes had been up to. Now he tried again.

"Take the first letter," he said.   "You state on the second page: 'I do hope that if we have to do some time on this thing that Jack, you and me can be together somewhere.' Why did you say that, Mr. Barnes?"

"Well, obviously this whole letter is a fabrication," Barnes replied.   "I am trying to use it as a means to an end."

Mr Merkle: *Which is what?*

Andrew Barnes: *To gain information.*

Mr. Merkle: *That's not true, is it Mr. Barnes?   That's not the reason for that letter.*

Andrew Barnes: *Well, no, it's not totally....*

Mr Merkle: *Did you want to spend time with Mr. Lehder and Mr. Reed?*

Andrew Barnes: *No, I didn't.*

Mr. Merkle: *You say further in that letter: 'You have my promise, and I will be riding down the path you make....' Now, you never indicated to me that you would not testify against Mr. Lehder. Is that correct?*

Andrew Barnes: *That's correct.*

Mr Merkle: *Why did you assure Mr. Lehder that you would not waver from the path he had made? Why did you want him to think that?*

Andrew Barnes: *I think it's plainly obvious. I wanted to pick Carlos's brain. I wanted to wrest as much information as I could about my case.*

Mr Merkle: *You haven't told the jury yet what the other reason was.*

Andrew Barnes: *I really have no response to it.*

And after all Robert Merkle's efforts, that was the best he could do. Short of a direct leading question, Andrew Barnes was not going to give him the answer he sought.

But in order to ask such a question, Merkle would have to know the answer already. And clearly he did not.

He made one more attempt: "You have admitted here to this jury that you did not love or miss Carlos Lehder very much. Correct?"

Andrew Barnes: *Correct.*

Mr Merkle: *Your wife did not miss Carlos Lehder very much.*

Andrew Barnes: *Correct.*

Mr. Merkle: *Little Andy...?*

Andrew Barnes: *Correct.*

Mr Merkle: *Why did you find it necessary to recount to Mr. Lehder the false proposition that your family your wife and your children loved and missed him, and that you would do nothing against him?*

Andrew Barnes: *Well, I was making a plea with the government at the time, and there were security matters at hand. But I still don't understand what you are driving at.*

Mr Merkle: *What do you mean by "security matters at hand"?*

Andrew Barnes: *Personal security.*

Mr Merkle: *You still can't give us any other reason why you wrote this letter?*

Andrew Barnes: *No, I really can't.*

*   *   *   *

There was a clue in Andrew Barnes' answers. Merkle was very close, but not quite close enough. The Englishman had indeed been concerned about his security and that of his family. What he did not say, and what he was never asked, was what assurances Carlos Lehder had made on the subject.

Messrs. Shohat and Quinon must have been mightily relieved about this. It could have been an embarrassment for the court to learn Barnes' interpretation of the message conveyed to him at the meeting of February 8.

According to Barnes, in a taped interview given after the Lehder trial and before he himself was sentenced, the message was simple: "Shohat indicated that Carlos would help me financially if I didn't testify against him. He would keep my family and kids alive."

This was a serious allegation. In effect, Barnes was accusing Lehder's lawyers of conniving at a bribery attempt. Later, questioned more closely, he modified his story. "It was not spelled out like that," he admitted to me. "It wasn't an actual money situation. But it was definitely relayed to me that if I chose to I could go that route (to stand trial and not testify against Lehder) and I could be assured that my family would be taken care of. It was conveyed to me that Carlos would look favourably upon me if I didn't testify against him. They clearly indicated that."

Whatever that carefully-phrased offer actually meant, Andrew Barnes had no doubt about what he thought it meant. And that was the true purpose of the extraordinary letters: to find out if Carlos really intended to help him out. In point of fact, although he got no reply, Barnes was sure that the Colombian would have been true to his word. "I'm sure Carlos would have looked after my family if I had refused to testify."

But in the end he decided to turn down the offer, if offer it was, and to testify instead. Not to do so would have meant pleading not guilty, standing trial, and facing the prospect of a very lengthy jail sentence. The improved plea-bargain deal from Robert Merkle, which arrived fortuitously before he had made up his mind, was the final factor that turned the scale.

"It's kind of a double-edged sword when you deal with things like this," he explained. "I was convinced that I wasn't betraying Carlos by testifying against him. The boat was already sunk. I wasn't going to do a hundred plus months either. I knew very well that if I had a seven-year cap I would probably get a 24-month sentence, actual time. That makes a hell of a lot of difference."

* * * *

Knowing nothing of this in the Jacksonville courthouse, lacking the information to ask the one question that would clarify everything, Robert Merkle was left flogging a dead horse. He lashed it a little while longer, angrily.

Mr Merkle: *Isn't it a fact that you told the government that you were terrified of Mr. Lehder?*

Jose Quinon was instantly on his feet. "Objection," he shouted. This was coming much too close to the bone.

"Your honour, it's true," said Merkle as the embattled attorneys reached the judge's side. "The fact of the matter is that this is right on point. They brought his state of mind up on this letter. They elicited a false explanation from him. He is repeatedly evading and dodging. He can't give an answer.

"In fact, he told government agents that he wanted the Witness Protection Programme. He was very concerned about his wife and children, and that goes to the very heart of what they suggest is a false proposition here. And in fact he is terrified.

"There's no magic involved here. I don't have to be a magician to advise the court that the witness told me he was extremely concerned about the safety of his wife and children. The court will recall the incident when Mr. Lehder made an obscene gesture to the witness, and how upset by that the witness was. As late as Thursday, the witness inquired if it was safe to go out to his car.

"The fact of the matter is, that this has been a continuing concern of the witness, up to the point where, when he initially agreed to co-operate with us, he had to talk long and hard with his wife to convince her it was the best course of conduct.

"Now obviously, the testimony on cross-examination elicited false statements: that what he was trying to do was to see Mr. Lehder, record conversations, and therefore put him in the position to get a better deal."

But the judge ruled against the U.S. Attorney, and the question was withdrawn. Instead, Merkle asked Barnes: "Why did you want Mr. Lehder to believe that your wife loved him and wanted to visit him?"

The exchange at sidebar had given the Englishman time to think. He came up with an answer worthy of Machiavelli. "This letter," he said, "with my home address and telephone number on it, basically ensures that no matter what happens to me as far as sentencing goes, the U.S. government has no choice but to take care of my family via the federal Witness Protection Programme."

Now why hadn't he thought of that before?

Mad Dog Merkle gave up. In his closing statement to the jury, he assured them that Andrew Barnes would go to jail for the full seven years. Perhaps he wished it could be more.

CHAPTER EIGHTEEN
Judgment

After a trial that lasted seven and a half months, all of it taken up with the prosecution case, Carlos Lehder Rivas was convicted on May 19, 1988, for conspiracy to smuggle 3.3 tons of cocaine into the United States. It was, curiously enough, almost exactly the same amount for which Andrew Barnes had been personally responsible. He offered no evidence in his defence, but even so the jury took several days to reach a verdict. On July 20, 1988, Judge Howell W. Melton sentenced him to the maximum possible term in jail: life without parole, plus 135 years. Plus a fine of $350,000.

Andrew Barnes' own moment of truth had come six days earlier. After several postponements, his sentencing hearing was finally set for July 14 in Court No 1, U.S. District Court, Jacksonville, at 1.30 p.m. I duly drove down to Florida to witness the last act in the drama. In fact the sentencing was transferred at the last minute to the smaller, more austere, Courtroom No 3, and I might have missed it had Judge Melton not been almost half an hour late in taking his seat on the bench.

Barnes can have taken little comfort from the knowledge that he was about to be sentenced by the same judge who had ruled over the Carlos Lehder trial. Though he had pleaded guilty, and there was thus to be no evidence presented and no trial, the slight figure on the bench knew everything he had done, down to the smallest detail.   It had all come out in the witness box in his testimony against Lehder.   Whether or not this affected the judge's decision is a moot point.   At all events, the tension in the sparse courtroom was palpable as the participants waited his pleasure.

At the insistence of his lawyer, Andrew Barnes had brought his entire family to court, in an attempt to create the right impression.   They sat in the public gallery at the rear; Barbara Barnes pale and drawn, lipstick slashed across her mouth like a bleeding wound; the two elder children neat and unsmiling.   Only little Katey, her pretty face scarred by a recent dog-bite, was careless and uncomprehending of what was about to happen.   She played and scrambled and fidgeted like any two-year-old, and once had to be removed by her mother when she burst out crying for no apparent reason. Andy Jr., "the world's youngest drug smuggler", now aged 12, sat upright and silent.   They might have been any American family fom any suburban neighbourhood. But they were not.

Barnes himself was calm, and seemingly confident before the hearing began.   Dressed in a camel-coloured sports jacket and sober tie, his grey flannel trousers neatly pressed and his mop of prematurely-greying hair freshly barbered, he chatted amiably with lawyers, DEA agents and friends at the back of the court.   When he stood to receive his sentence, he dwarfed the slight figure of his attorney, Russell Healey.

The proceedings were brief. Healey raised a few nit-picking objections with the judge over the court record, got nowhere, and called his first and only character witness: Barbara Barnes. Barbara, her loose cotton dress of pink and green hanging like some penitent's robe, did not waste too many words on her errant spouse.

"I would just like to say on Andy's behalf," she said, "that he has been a good husband and father to the children, and they are very close to him. He has made a conscious effort to change his life around." And that was all.

Russell Healey was somewhat more loquacious, but exhibited all the passion and fire in defence of his client of a reluctant schoolboy reciting a boring poem by a declining Wordsworth. "Barnes describes himself as '32 going on 52,'" he said, "and I am sure the court, after hearing his six or so days of testimony in the Lehder trial, will understand that.

"Barnes stands before the court with not a lot of positive things having occurred. The positive things are his wife and three children. They are standing by him and are very supportive of him. He has made a serious effort to turn his life around."

Russell Healey went on to describe, not entirely accurately, his client's role in informing on John Torres. "He initiated contact with law enforcement," he said. "He realised he was running the risk of losing the only things of value he had left - his wife and family. It is significant to note that he put himself in jeopardy in regard to the extensive testimony in this court. And by wearing a bug in relation to Torres. Not only did he agree to be wired; he engaged Torres in conversations which were videotaped as well. It shows a large amount of courage and virtue on behalf of Mr. Barnes to go to that length to terminate completely any possible further contact with these people.

"I think it would be fair to say that Mr. Barnes' co-operation was extremely important, and he has played a major role as far as the conviction of Carlos Lehder was concerned. In view of the unparalleled co-operation he has given, I would ask the court to be as lenient as possible, to allow him to hope to do the only thing he can do that is important to him at this moment - and that is to keep his family together.

"Throughout the time I have represented Mr. Barnes, the constant theme has been that he wanted to do whatever was necessary, so that he could be with his children when they grew up."

Andrew Barnes' attachment to a united family was, and is, an undeniable fact. The trouble was that in the past it had taken the form of involving them in smuggling cocaine. And the judge knew it.

Now it was his turn to speak in his own defense. Like Barbara, he wasted few words. The delivery was flat and devoid of emotion; lawyer's words, not his own. "I just want to express to the court my deep remorse for the rimes I have committed," said Andrew Barnes. "I offer no excuses. I have none. You heard the testimony from my wife. We are trying to stand together and work this thing out. I would just like to express my regrets. That is all."

Judge Melton looked down at him like a man who had heard that speech before. Which he probably had. Many times. Then he listened impassively while counsel on both sides whispered secretly in his ear about on-going investigations in which Barnes was involved.

Then it was time for the prosecution, in the person of Ernst Mueller, to have its say. Before the hearing, Barnes had been confident that the Assistant U.S. Attorney would not demand the maximum sentence. But would he? Tension in the court increased.

As it turned out, Ernst Mueller gave a more eloquent display on behalf of Andrew Barnes than his own attorney had achieved. "Since the time Mr. Barnes has been in this case," he said, "he has been co-operating as much as possible. I would say the government has imposed on him as much as it can on anyone in these circumstances. Basically, he has been working almost full time for the government, and doing so without being paid - in the sense that the only moneys he has received are witness fees relating to his appearances in court.

"His crime is a serious one. None the less, I think he has done everything possible to mitigate it. His testimony was an important contribution in securing the conviction of Carlos Lehder, and the indictment of Torres and seven others is a direct result of Barnes' co-operation. Torres is certainly a very significant drug dealer, and the FBI regards this as a very important case. I think it is not unfair to say that Barnes' co-operation involved a certain amount of personal risk, and will continue to do so.

"The people who were going to buy the drugs were the organised crime family of Pennsylvania - members of the Gambino family - so Mr. Barnes was in serious jeopardy from them, as well as from Torres himself, in addition to any risk that might arise from the Lehder case.

"Finally, he is co-operating with an investigation in the Bahamas. There are three public officials there under investigation, and it is anticipated that he will have to testify in the Bahamas, and that he will continue to co-operate in this and other criminal cases.

"In terms of quality and importance, his co-operation has been of the highest possible level. It is my view that in the light of that co-operation, although the court could impose up to seven years, it should impose a lesser sentence than Mr. Barnes' offence seems to deserve.

"We would propose a sentence of not more than four or five years."

Seen from the rear, Andrew Barnes' shoulders lifted perceptibly. But Judge Melton seemed unimpressed. "How do you equate that with Mr. Merkle's statement in the Lehder case that Barnes would serve seven years?" he asked Mueller. "How do you justify the difference between what you recommend and what the U.S. Attorney stated in his argument to the jury?"

Robert Merkle would never have said that, replied the prosecutor, if he had known the extent of Andrew Barnes' co-operation with the authorities. The former smuggler had gone well beyond the terms in his plea bargain agreement. "It is my view that when this sort of thing occurs, which is not very common, it ought to have some reward," he said. Because of the sentencing guidelines, Mueller added, Barnes would have to serve virtually every day of whatever sentence was imposed.

At first, Judge Melton seemed receptive to the argument. "Barnes is a young man, and obviously very intelligent," he said. "Obviously he has love for his family, and they for him. I think he was an excellent witness. He showed a great deal of intelligence in being able to present his testimony. He is obviously a man with a great deal of ability."

But that was the limit of the judge's generosity. Barnes, he said, had been very much involved in drug smuggling, and but for the plea bargain could have faced sentences of fifteen years on multiple counts.

"It gives me concern," he went on. "I remember his testimony about how he got involved in this. It was essentially money that was the motive. But it is the beggar at the end of the line who ultimately provides that money, and takes whatever risk they have to to get it."

Then the blow fell. "Because of that," said Judge Melton, "I cannot go below seven years in this case." Then he allowed Andrew Barnes to remain free without bond for ninety days, so that he could continue to give the co-operation that had just benefited him so little. Barnes gave a wry smile.

The judge rose. Having just imposed the harshest sentence at his command, he said something rather surprising.

"Good luck to you, Mr. Barnes," said Judge Howell Melton. "I hope it works out."

EPILOGUE

Robert Merkle had been instrumental in getting Andrew Barnes a maximum jail sentence. It was typical of the Englishman that he bore the former U.S. attorney no ill will. All the same, he was surprised when a letter from Merkle's election campaign dropped in his post-box a few days after the sentencing hearing, and to find that he was being invited to contribute to the campaign funds of his nemesis. Merkle, running on a law and order platform for the Republican Senate nomination in Florida, was seeking support from the very criminals he had convicted.

Andrew Barnes gave the matter some thought, and decided not to subscribe. Charity had its limits, even for him. As a matter of record, the Republican primary election was held on September 6, 1988. Robert Merkle lost.

Under the terms of his sentencing, Barnes remained free for 90 days. He spent much of the time continuing to help the FBI investigation of the Torres operation in Miami, and the inquiry into high-level corruption in the Bahamas. For some time he clung to the hope that legal moves to get his sentence set aside might succeed. But despite the tacit support of government attorneys they came to nothing.

He was given the choice of serving his seven years in one of two "country club" prisons, one in Allenwood, Pennsylvania, and the other at Lompoc, California.

"They are none the less JAIL!" he wrote to me in a letter dated August 12, 1988.   "I have chosen the latter on account of two factors:

1) Gambino does not control Lompoc, and

2) Ivan Boesky and his gang live there - maybe I can learn something from these guys!"

On the misty fall morning of October 15, 1988, Andrew Richard Barnes kissed his family good-bye and set off across America to California and incarceration. The long journey that began in a Colombian farmyard was finally over.

SynergEbooks

™

Taking Books to New Heights!